D0933234

ANOTHER GUIDE TO RPG STORYTELLING

FROM DREAM TO DICE

ARON CHRISTENSEN

LOOSE LEAF
STORIES

Copyright © 2018
Aron Christensen
and Loose Leaf Stories
All rights reserved
ISBN: 9781643190501 (KDP) &
9781643190495 (IngramSpark)

Cover art by Tithi Luadthong
Edited by Erica Lindquist,
Amber Presley, and Lacey Waymire

This book and its author are not associated with any
specific role-playing game company or system.

Find more of my books at LLStories.com

CONTENTS

INTRODUCTION

Hello again! Back for more?

I spent the first Storytelling guide and then the companion discussing the methods and tools that I use for running table-top role-playing games. In this third volume, I'll take each of those pieces and actually put them together into an RPG – from the initial game concept to final execution and then a detailed post-mortem on each campaign session.

There are lots of ways to role-play and just as many books about each one – this is just *my* take on the process and experience. And so far, I've never gamed with a group that does it quite the same way I do. Hopefully I have something new or interesting to share.

This book is meant to serve as an example and case study about how I build a game so that you can create your own. We'll start with the game concept and a little world-building, then break the story idea down into discrete pieces which I'll expand into the finished chapters that I use to run my game.

After that, I'll actually run the game for my group and tell you how that went, including commentary about how I adapted when my players did something unexpected, how I changed things on the fly, or had to course-correct when I screwed up.

If that all sounds complicated, don't worry – it's really not. We'll just take this thing one step at a time until we turn a simple story idea into a complete role-playing game.

GETTING STARTED

Running a game set in one of the Dungeons & Dragons worlds or another copyrighted setting is just fine within your own group. But in order to publish a guide running you through the process, I'll need to use a setting that won't get my ass sued. Luckily, my wife and I are writers and have built worlds for our own novels – so we'll use one of those. The chances of me suing myself are pretty low.

For this game, I picked out *Tydalus*. It's a story and setting that we haven't published yet, but that has been on our to-do list for a couple of years. We'll end up doing a lot of world-building for the game, which I expect will get us excited enough to bump the novel up our list, but that doesn't matter for the role-playing game. What matters here is that I can walk you through how I built the world, and the differences between creating for a novel and a role-playing game.

The world of Tydalus is inspired by what some have named the *Mythos* – the collected works of H.P. Lovecraft and a lot of talented authors who built on and expanded his ideas. But rather than set my story in Lovecraft's early twentieth century or our own modern era, I wanted to take the Mythos back to an archaic fantasy setting. Most of the Mythos elements are public domain, so I was free to draw heavily upon specific monsters and characters, but it's the theme I'm really after: horrors from deep below the earth, doom descending from the stars, and evil beyond human comprehension. Fun stuff like that.

If you like the setting and game that I put together here, please feel free to use or run it yourself. Just don't publish anything using Tydalus. Chances are pretty good that neither of us can afford to go to court over it, but let's not find out.

One of the other things I can get my butt sued for misusing are copyrighted game systems. So just like the other storytelling guides, I won't be using any system-specific rolls or terminology. Whatever RPG system you usually play doubtlessly has its own dice and rules manuals to cover all of that. I really don't have much to add to the dice-rolling part of RPGs – mostly I'm going to be talking about how to give a game a narrative shot of adrenalin.

Regardless of your system, Tydalus will introduce a necessary mechanic for any Mythos game – sanity. Most RPGs don't include it, so you may need to adapt something to fit. In this case, sanity will be a pool used to resist mind-shattering horrors and which will be slowly worn down until the characters begin going mad.

I've used sanity mechanics in several RPG systems before, when simply seeing things not meant to be witnessed by the human mind inflicts trauma. When I told my players to roll their perception or alertness, they groaned and asked if their characters could just squeeze their eyes shut and not look. Ignorance truly is bliss.

In the Mythos – and the broader genre, sometimes called *cosmic horror* – monsters are real. But this isn't epic or high fantasy, where those monsters can be found in any forest and fought with magic swords for morning exercise. Tydalus is a pre-industrial world in which very few people are aware of the dimensions and powers far stranger than their own, and those rare initiates into the mysteries know to fear them.

With that basic premise out on the table, let's do some world-building for Tydalus.

Fair warning – it's a long section. I hope that it will help make sense of what I'm doing when I begin developing the story. But if it feels like information overload right now, you can just skip up to Chapter 4, and then come back to world-building later, when you already have a sense of the story I'm going to tell.

WORLD-BUILDING

Groundwork

Let's figure out the setting for my game. I have a simple idea for the plot, but it only works because this novel concept has been on our to-write list for a while and I know a bit about the world. So let me catch you up on some of the basics, and then we'll flesh it out as we go. Since we haven't written out the Tydalus novel yet, a lot of these ideas are still vague and will need some work.

Tydalus is an ocean-bound world – probably around eighty percent water – with the land broken up into islands and a few small continents. A very large, high-mass moon on a long elliptical orbit passes close enough to the planet every few generations to cause the ocean tide to rise up thousands of feet, submerging all but the highest elevations. As a result, human civilizations cling to mountaintop city-states, which turn into islands during high tide. And when the tide is high, horrors from deep below the sea rise up to prey upon humanity.

Because I want monsters and magic to be strange and incomprehensible in this setting, the mystic stuff has to be rare. This is a low-magic setting – that means few wizards or blessed clerics, no magic shops or enchanted swords. The heroes of Tydalus are just people with iron wills and keen minds, willing and able to confront ancient evils, to risk their lives and sanity to save humanity from cosmic horrors.

We have our big moon to bring the high tide every few hundred years or so, but we don't want these tides to be the only ones. So I'm going to add some more moons to push and pull the vast oceans of Tydalus. The other moons aren't as big and don't come as close, so they won't have as drastic an effect on the sea, but they'll allow me to give the world normal daily tides.

Then how many moons does Tydalus have? No more than five because I don't want to have to keep track of too many. So let's do three moons – the big one and then two smaller satellites. In combination, they give us lots of options for regular tides. Their interactions would be reasonably complicated, so we can have tides go in and out whenever we want and a player would have to make a chart to catch me in an inconsistency.

I debated whether to name each of the moons, number them, or simply call them by colors. Numbers or colors (First Moon, the Red Moon, and so on) are simple and easy to remember. It's not a great idea to make your players memorize too many weird names, especially if they're not important for the game – which they're not for this campaign. Tydalus is a world that my group has never played in before, and they're going to have a lot to learn anyway.

So I decided to give the three moons names that would play into the mythology – which I'll get to in a moment – but be easy enough for my players to remember. The moons are the Mother, the Father, and the Grandfather. Guess which one causes the big, evil high tide? This is also a nod to Lovecraft's Mother Hydra, Father Dagon, and Cthulhu – whose position in the unholy trinity lies vaguely above the other two. Maybe ancient Tydalus texts even name the

moons *Mother Dra, Father Dag,* and *Grandfather Ctlu* or something...
But the familial titles are enough to give the moons some personality without overwhelming my players with information.

Alright, now we have big oceans and a couple of moons. Next, I
need to think about the land of Tydalus. The whole world can't be
made up of mountains, but we ran into a problem with the lowlands. If there are plains between the mountains, and the high tide
that covers the land only comes every few generations, then why
don't people spend fifty years farming the shit out of it in between
tides? It's just not believable that the people of this world wouldn't
use whatever land they could.

And so I decided that there aren't many plains in this world at
all. Take that, plains! Instead, I'll make Tydalus a highly tectonically
active planet, which makes seventy-five percent of the landmasses
mountainous, and the few lowlands spend so much time under the
salty ocean waters that they have become largely inhospitable to
crops. Now farming is done on terraces and in a few high mountain
valleys. During the huge Grandfather tide, the valleys and the lower
terraces are flooded and any peasants working there either retreat
up the mountain or are abandoned to drown.

Culture and civilization

What's the culture of Tydalus like? The standard pseudo-European
medieval fare? That's a start, but it's been done to death and often
problematically. Besides, I want to make my game world a bit more
interesting than that.

I established a bit of world lore for the novel, so let's start there.
The Tydalus books call for a series of lighthouses that guard the
coast and the ocean, and then people to staff them. Those lighthouses and their inhabitants are going to be important for my game
idea, too, so figuring out why they exist is vital.

I took a look into Tydalus' history. Sure, I could just arbitrarily decide the shape of things and say *because reasons*. But creating a solid history for your game world will ground the whole story and campaign, making it feel that much more immersive. Plus, filling out the setting's history often uncovers neat ideas that I wouldn't otherwise have considered.

Let's get in there and figure out the history of Tydalus. A good starting place in the cosmic horror genre is that this planet doesn't belong to humanity and never has. Tydalus is the physical play-ground of unknowable elder gods and other old, bad things. Those ancient horrors are taking a *really* long nap right now, and while they're not paying attention, other species have evolved and built their own civilizations. These foolish little creatures think they rule Tydalus... And the most successful of them weren't even human.

Entire races have risen, flourished on Tydalus, then died out or been destroyed. Maybe one of the elder gods rolled over in their sleep. Maybe the Grandfather tide drowned a whole civilization. Perhaps these precursors destroyed themselves or were overthrown by their successors. The point is that humans are only the latest in a long line of species to inhabit the world of Tydalus and think them-selves its master while Cthulhu hits the cosmic snooze button.

Just five more eons, Mom!

In order to give my game setting the sense of history that I want, let's start three civilizations back – probably the earliest species of Tydalus that could be fairly called *human*. These people spread over most of the planet's dry land and held onto it long enough to create an advanced civilization. They developed magic or tech-nology – at a certain point, the two become hard to distinguish – far beyond the understanding of Tydalus' current inhabitants. That is, the characters that my players will be controlling in this campaign.

But the first people got pretty messed up. Their arts and tech-nology were advanced, but they also became dangerously decadent.

The very worst Roman emperors had nothing on these guys. They inbred with Deep Ones from the sea – yep, fish-man orgies – and so what began as decadence turned into degeneration.

The people of Tydalus devolved into cruel monster hybrids who worshiped blasphemies on blood- and salt-stained altars, making sacrifices to nightmare-inducing idols of ancient evils best left to their slumber. Hmm... That's not bad. I might use that description during game.

That's just the first civilization in my lineup, though. So let's start on the second one... They lived on a more southern equatorial continent, but their numerous mountains were volcanic – and quite active. Not exactly a safe place to hide from the high tides, but this civilization were ship-builders and sailors, and a significant number of them decided *screw these ash-spewing fire-mountains* and went in search of somewhere they didn't have to choose between drowning and red-hot magma.

Moving north, they found the main continent where my game will take place. It was larger and less volcanic, with lots of stable mountains already terraced for farming – all occupied by the first civilization, which had fallen into barbarism.

The second civilization did what colonists do – declare war and claim the conquered land for themselves. To be fair to our second wave of humans, the first ones were seriously evil. And barely even human anymore, so they drove the fish-people hybrids west and into the sea. Then the new humans built over all of the creepy first-civilization stuff, and claimed the continent for their own.

Alright, that gives us some horrifying buried cities left over from the fish-men, fodder for stories and games about long-abandoned temples and forgotten chambers hidden in otherwise innocuous places. Great, that's some useful stuff.

Now it's time to deal with those lighthouses that I want along the coast. They are meant to be scout- and guard-posts against the terrors that still lurk out there in the ocean. The second major civilization pushed the monsters that came before them west into the sea, and then built these lighthouses to guard against their return.

At first, I was thinking that they were only slightly bigger than the lighthouses we're all familiar with. But if the tides that drown the land are high enough to turn mountaintops into islands, then these lighthouses will have to be a lot bigger to avoid drowning. So now we're talking about towers that stand thousands of feet tall, with massive infrastructure to support them. That's a steep architecture order, so I'm going to add a footnote that they had to use ships to float and then sink great stone blocks into place during high tides in order to build these behemoths.

With their western coast safeguarded against the horrors of the deep, dark ocean, Civilization Two ruled the continent for several centuries. They watched the west for monsters, but their problem came from the east. Which leads me to Civilization Three.

In the east, I placed a vast green steppe land across the ocean, and the humans there lived safely above the tides. But remember when I made Tydalus a tectonically active world? That's because I want to bring down this continent with a series of terrible earthquakes that suddenly dropped the average elevation low enough to be drowned by the hungry ocean.

A significant portion of the humans living on the eastern continent died during the quakes, and the tide was rushing in to wipe out the other half. So as many people as were able hurried north and followed a half-frozen land bridge to reach the more mountainous lands in the west. The land bridge was washed out and destroyed behind them by more earthquakes, forcing the refugees to make a home on this new continent.

Unfortunately for both sides of the coming conflict, this new land was already occupied by Civilization Two, and neither group was interested in sharing.

The second civilization and the new flood of refugees went to war over ownership of the mountains. Civilization Two had experience with ships and water-based warfare, but that didn't help much when the newcomers invaded their dry mountaintops.

Civilization Three brought horses and dogs from their homeland, too, which serve them far better in the bloody war. Plus, they were desperate. They don't have a home to return to.

So these new humans swiftly took control of a couple mountains, and then spread out all across the continent. Over the next generation or so, Civilization Three invaded and took over the new continent, driving Civilization Two further and further west until they were forced into the lighthouses.

While these coastal fortresses were difficult to assault, the third civilization would have eventually starved them out, but the Grandfather tide was still rising and soon even the new mountains were drowning, turning into islands.

The altered and very wet landscape changed absolutely everything. Civilization Three had been traveling by land for centuries and didn't know much about sailing – to say nothing of the monsters swimming in with the Grandfather tide. That left the war-torn remains of Civilization Two to fight off their old enemies, and the new colonists swiftly reconsidered their plan to destroy the coastal lighthouses and their occupants.

When the high tide finally went out again, the two human civilizations called a truce. Civilization Three cut Two a deal – you get the coast and your lighthouses, but you have to keep the icky, scary things in the sea away. The coastal cliffs aren't arable, so we'll send you food from our farm terraces.

This wasn't a good deal and pretty much turned Civilization Two's lighthouses into an expendable buffer zone, but they didn't have much choice. With the high tide in retreat once more, they lost their strategic advantage. So in order to survive, Civilization Two agreed to these unfair terms, and Civilization Three became the dominant power in the land. They paved over their predecessors' cities, burying the first civilization that much deeper.

And that's the shape of things in the era where I plan to set my game. We have a dominant culture occupying most of the mainland, with a smaller and older civilization living on the west coast. They're still a seafaring culture, people willing to do crazy shit like go fishing and travel by boat during the high tide.

So Civilization Two is a badass society, but a vanishing one... Between wars with the newcomers and the monsters that came with the tide, their population was decimated. There aren't enough to repopulate their numbers, and interbreeding with Civilization Three is thinning their bloodlines.

The civilization which currently dominates the land is a group of city-states, each claiming one of the highest mountaintops and a few nearby peaks. While all of these people originally came from the same continent, generations separated across isolated mountains have resulted in several diverging cultures. Imagine the city-states of Greece – Athens and Sparta were both Greek nations, but had wildly different cultures.

I've decided on thirteen of these city-states. It feels like a manageable number, but a large enough one to create variety. Besides, thirteen is supposed to be an unlucky number and the characters in this game are going to be very, very unlucky.

That's as much history as I'm going to develop right now. When we get into the game outline, I'll expand on the bits that my story interacts with or places my player characters want to come from.

Miscellaneous stuff

There are a few other details that I want to include in the world of Tydalus. Some major plot points, some nit-picky little details.

First, there are salt mines all along the coast. Salt is vitally important in any setting without refrigeration for food preservation.

Mining the salt is hard and dangerous, so it's primarily done by prisoners. And with the constant danger of unspeakable monsters from the sea, being sent to those mines along the western ocean is about the worst punishment on Tydalus.

The prisoners are criminals sent from the mountain city-states. Since the inlanders fear the sea, it's considered a punishment. That means it's the job of the lighthouse keepers to both protect the prisoners and keep them in line. The intermingling that is diluting the second civilization's bloodline is primarily with these prisoners.

One of the other set pieces that I came up with for the novels is an inland sea – basically a gigantic tide pool that fills during each high tide with the sort of horrors that haunt the ocean. That sea might give me some other game opportunities if I want to deal with monsters far from the coast. Not sure if I'll use it in this campaign.

Another early idea was that Civilization One – the humans who devolved into fish-men – built a huge, magnificent artificial mountain to be their capital city. It was a massive, epically-scaled ziggurat located in more or less the center of the continent. Over the eons, earth has built up and erosion has ground down the sharp edges. Civilization Two built over the first cities, and then Civilization Three did the same thing. By now, the ancient capital ziggurat is no longer distinguishable from the other terraced mountains of the mainland. But it's still there...

To the lighthouse keepers, it's all a hazy memory – "the altars that we broke and the atrocities committed upon them" – and most people have entirely forgotten that the mountain isn't natural. Who knows what sealed chambers and buried lore lie under the sediment of two civilizations and thousands of years?

The rest of Tydalus' land masses can just remain vague, to be honest. The volcanic southern islands, the sunken eastern steppes, and whatever else lies to the west and north doesn't really matter right now. If it's not a part of the game I intend to run, detailing it too much will just take time away from developing the story for my players.

That does remind me that I have a bit of an idea about the far north, though. Not for land masses, but what's to stop the humans from moving up into the snowy places? These people have developed coat technology, after all. But the skies of Lovecraft's Mythos are almost as full of horrors as the sea, and I want to mirror that in Tydalus. So I've filled the cold northern sky with madness-inducing auroras – the burning lights that are the breath of the elder gods or something. No one can look at them and remain sane.

I'm pretty sure I can use that somewhere in my story.

Alright, let's do a few last bits of basic world-building to fill in the cracks before we dig into my story idea. The game is going to be based pretty heavily in the world lore of Tydalus, so trust me that this work is all worth doing ahead of time.

The mountains and seas of Tydalus are going to shape the flora and fauna of that world. I'm not envisioning a lot of plains animals like bison, but there should be plenty of fish and whales, dolphins and seagulls. Up in the mountains will be hawks and eagles, goats, sheep and cougars. Goat meat and milk are probably a major staple of any human diet on Tydalus.

Humans domesticated mountain lions into smaller cats, which are useful for protecting food stores from rodents – and those grain stores will be incredibly important during high tides, when a lot of farming terraces vanish beneath the waves. A quick Google search for the best calorie yield per acre suggests that potatoes and corn are the most efficient crops, so those are the main farming products on Tydalus.

Our third civilization brought horses from the steppes, but while they're strong and fast, horses also need a lot of grassland that just isn't available on the new continent. So horses will be rare and kept mostly for the use of the rich or those who are willing to pay a lot of money for speed.

Fish are an excellent source of protein, but Civilization Three fears water. That leaves fishing to the lighthouse keepers, who have maintained their boating and seafaring traditions even now. The sea isn't a friendly place, however, and they tend to catch a lot of freaky creatures – pilot fish and oversized squid that wander into the shallow water. The things that live in the deep oceanic trenches of Tydalus are a whole other level of scary shit.

That's plenty for an RPG world, full of dangerous and frightening possibilities. Alright, maybe corn isn't scary, but it took just a few minutes to add that detail and now I know a lot more about this world. Between Tydalus' tectonic activity and tides, I can move the mountains, and cover or uncover them as needed. And as this land's latest inhabitants carve new terraces and storage caverns into their mountains, who knows what secrets they may unearth?

Naming things

Now we have a place for humans to live, some animals for them to domesticate, and food for them to eat. But that means it's time to start naming things. I can't keep calling people *Civilization Three*. Placeholder names are only going to work for so long, and I might as well start giving everything their proper names.

Ugh... I suck at coming up with names, so I hit Google Translate a lot. If my inspiration is Hungarian, I look up the Hungarian translation for *bad guy* and that's the base I use for naming my main antagonist. My players rarely know what I'm up to, but those translations don't always work well as names. And it can be insensitive to the culture that I took inspiration from, especially if they're a marginalized group. Go ahead and be inspired by other languages, but don't just steal their words.

Name generators can be useful tools, but they're often not very consistent when I'm going for a certain sense of cultural cohesion in my game world, which is why I use translations in the first place.

So for Tydalus, I'm turning to my secret weapon – my wife and coauthor, Erica. She *is* a random name generator, except without the random part. There are plenty of skills that I bring to our games and novels, but she's the one with a flair for naming people, places and things with a distinct but consistent flavor.

Tydalus is the name of the planet that my story will take place on, and the general name for the setting. But the main continent will need a name of its own, which Erica has decided will be called Korvath. That's where all of the action is going to happen.

For the first civilization, the once-advanced but now fallen fishmen, I wanted a name right out of Lovecraft's Mythos. We decided to call them the Cthyan (kuh-THEE-an) Empire, with the *Cth* from *Cthulhu*. We named the Cthyans' artificial mountain and capital city *Arkhest* in honor of *Arkham* from Lovecraft's stories.

Civilization Two is the seafaring one. In our real-world history, some of the most famous sailors were the Vikings, Polynesians, and various European nations during the Age of Exploration. Especially with the volcanoes that forced Civilization Two from their home, we were most inspired by the Polynesian explorers, so we've collectively named Civilization Two's abandoned islands *Sulaweya*.

What about the people from Sulaweya? Not every society takes its name from the place they live, so Erica suggested calling them the Kelanua. I liked the sound of that, and it shortens nicely to Kels – as in "those damned crazy Kels" when people are being assholes to them. And I figured that the Kelanua gave their own names to things in Korvath, too. So when they sacked the Cthyan Empire and drove the remnants of that civilization from the continent, the Kelanua took Arkhest and renamed it Arkhai'ah.

Great! Next, let's go on to Civilization Three. We've named their lost continent Antora, and their language is going to be very important, since theirs is the dominant culture in Korvath right now. I had them rename Arkhest/Arkhai'ah to Arkhome, both to make things easier for my players to pronounce and to provide a stark contrast to the Mythos-style tongue-twister names like *Nyarlathotep* and *Yog-Sothoth*.

I think the new civilization is made up of a couple groups, so I'll collectively call them the *Antorans*. The continent of Antora was less mountainous than Korvath, so that's going to shape the cultures that evolved there. The Antorans had more room and more independent nations, three of which managed the migration west into Korvath before their homes sank into the sea. These three groups combined to make up modern Antoran culture.

The first Antoran sub-culture I've come up with are the Strazni. They came from the cold, harsh northern reaches of Antora. Up to the north, the Strazni had those madness-inducing auroras, and the land bridge to the west. Ancient Cthyans used to raid Antora across that bridge, both during the height of the Cthyan Empire and then as they degenerated into barbarism. They took Strazni slaves, and also brought potatoes to Antora.

Alright, maybe that last bit about potatoes is a pointless detail, but I can get carried away with the world-building. It's a fun part of creating any game, but it can also be a bottomless rabbit hole. Don't get so carried away with creating the setting for your game that you never get back to building the story. All of this is just set dressing and background for your plot.

Back to the Strazni. The Cthyan raiders meant there was a little interbreeding between them and the Strazni. Not enough to result in major changes, but the Strazni have paler skin than the other races of Tydalus, and a higher percentage of blue or green eyes than the others. But since blue and green are colors reminiscent of the sea and the auroras, those eyes are considered by the Kelanua as a mark of ill luck or actual evil.

South of the Strazni were the vast steppes of Antora, where the largest number of its people lived. These broad, flat grasslands were an ideal place for horses and resulted in a flourishing culture of mounted raiders. Between constant raids from the west and south, the Strazni evolved a cultural siege mentality. Their primary exports were coldness and misery. To this day, the Strazni remain a hardy people who are accustomed to and usually expect hardship.

Erica named the steppe lands to the south *Bhataar*, and after a brief debate about the plural noun form, I've decided the Bhataari were a large group of nomadic tribes. We could get really granular about tribal variations, but unless one of the players wants their character to be a Bhataari with a strong connection to the old way, it's not really necessary for this game.

The Bhataari had the space and the horses to become expert mounted fighters. Because every fantasy setting has horse people. That's the rule. Bhataari were the first badasses on Tydalus to learn how to shoot bows and cut down peasants from horseback. They successfully raided the Strazni to the north and the Massir in the south for centuries. (More on the Massir in a minute.)

Every few hundred years, a warlord unified the Bhataari tribes and conquered bits of other kingdoms. But then the warlord would die in battle or of old age, and their children or grandchildren inevitably fought over rulership or just couldn't hold the new empire together, then it would break apart. So the Bhataari went through cycles of heavy raiding and conquest, followed by periods of relative peace and using their great mobility to facilitate trade before deciding that they should claim it all and begin raiding again.

Between their raiding and trade, the Bhataari were responsible for most of the cultural exchange across Antora. By borrowing a lot of Massir and a few Strazni words, they created a blended language that was adopted all across the continent as the de facto tongue of trade. When the Antorans were forced to cross the land bridge to escape their sinking homes and fight against the Kelanua for their new place in Korvath, this trade language became the backbone of the combined tongue now simply known as *Antoran*. Now the old Strazni, Massir and Bhataari dialects have faded and are secondary languages in most Antoran households.

Let's go on to the Massir. Their nation was located in southern Antora, straddling the equator. It was mostly desert, but on Tydalus, lack of water is more or less a good thing. There were a few dozen large oases that could support agriculture and as long as the Massir built their cities nearby, they flourished.

The deserts were hard going for Bhataari horses, which meant the Massir were raided less often than the Strazni. And the Massir even discovered that they could pay off most of the raiders, giving them some portion of what they would have stolen with no loss of life on either side.

Having to spend less time on food and safety meant more time for the Massir to develop the arts, math, and science. Astronomy is important on Tydalus, of course, what with the Grandfather Moon trying to drown the planet every few centuries. So the Massir were skilled stargazers, tracking the three moons and the other planets of the solar system. Their sandy deserts gave them access to silica for lenses and mirrors that led the Massir to develop the first telescopes on Tydalus. And the dry climate made it easy to store large collections of books without decay. Even in Tydalus' modern era, Massir is the language of scholars and learning.

There were a few other kingdoms on Antora, but none of them survived the sinking of the continent. The Strazni were closest to the land bridge, the Bhataari were the most mobile, and the Massir could accurately predict the coming of the Grandfather tide. I have some ideas for the religion of Tydalus and it surrounds the mythology of lost Antora, so that's as much of the big exodus as I'll detail right here.

These three cultures were thrown together when Antora was doomed, and they all fled west. A large percentage of their population doubtlessly died, but enough of them made it to Korvath to defeat the Kelanua. The Bhataari horses gave the Antorans a huge advantage – they could race out ahead of Kelanua reinforcements, and bows from horseback had far superior range compared to the thrown harpoons favored by the Kels.

In case it isn't obvious, I was inspired by the Mongolian tribes of Asia and the Muslim scholars of the Middle East when creating the Bhataari and the Massir. Between the intermingling of these three Antoran groups and less frequent interbreeding with the Kelanua, I hope that the population of Tydalus isn't just a homogenous fantasy world of European-style groups.

This backstory also gives me a list of primary languages. Just about everyone on Korvath speaks Antoran. As mentioned above, Strazni and Bhataari are less common dialects – mostly used by someone's grandma when they're pissed off. Massir is preserved a little more thoroughly in the schools, and particularly snooty works of scholarship are still written in the language.

The Kelanua have their own language, but that requires a little more thought. It's hard to carry libraries on a ship without getting them soggy and ruining the ink, but songs and stories are an excellent way to both entertain and educate while on the sea. So I think that even though most of the Kelanua have been forced by necessity to learn the hodgepodge language of their Antoran conquerors, they have preserved their own language through a strong oral tradition that goes all the way back to Sulaweya. It hasn't changed much since then.

What about the Cthyan language? The Cthyan Empire lasted a lot longer on Korvath than the Kelanua kingdom. How long the Antoran city-states survive remains to be seen...

But the Cthyans had a long enough history for their language to change substantially over the centuries, so I think that I'll break it out into Early, Middle and Late Cthyan. You know, like we have Old and Middle English. Middle Cthyan was the fish-man empire at its height, so it will be complex and beautiful... if a little creepy. Late Cthyan was spoken by the devolving remnants of that culture and

I'm imagining it as not much more than a complicated collection of grunts.

That gives me a good-sized and flavorful collection of languages to work with for this game. If the story or my players call for more granularity, I can always dip into the tribal dialects of the Bhataari or bring up languages that pre-date even the Cthyan Empire. If I need a book to be in some obscure language that none of the player characters speak, I think I'm covered.

Map!

This is an epic fantasy world that is wildly different from our own, and geography plays a big part in it. That means I pretty much have to create a map to help my players conceptualize it. Erica and I even made a literal back-of-the-napkin map while we were at dinner.

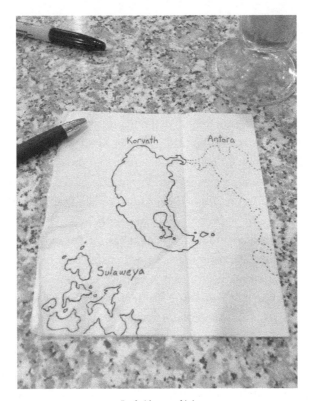

Look, it's a mapkin!

Erica gets credit for the map. I drew one, but it was way, way less attractive. She even placed the inland sea and put a dotted outline around Antora so you can tell it's sunken.

I don't know if we'll need the map during game, but at least I can show it to my players to give them some idea of what the world of Tydalus looks like.

Religion

Religion has a profound and powerful influence on any culture, so I'll need to sort out the spiritual history of Tydalus.

The Cthyan religion was the easiest to figure out. They worship the elder gods that are so iconic to Lovecraft's Mythos. I'a Cthulhu! For them, the Grandfather, Mother, and Father Moons were effectively Cthulhu, Hydra and Dagon. Maybe the gods themselves or just their personal realms... I'm not really sure, and I don't think it's going to matter for this game. We'll find out!

But the three moons should probably figure prominently in all of Tydalus' religions. They affect the planet far too drastically not to become major figures in the world's mythology. Because Grandfather Moon brings the tides and earthquakes as it pulls on Tydalus' tectonic plates, he's one hell of a dangerous god. He's going to be the destroyer in just about any religion that arises across the globe, smiting anything he disapproves of and raising new mountains out of the sea in their place.

The Mother and Father are kinder celestial figures who stand between Tydalus and the Grandfather Moon. But even they can be capricious and it's never wise to mess with the gods.

For the Kelanua, I decided on an animistic tradition. To them, Tydalus' moons represent the greatest and most powerful spirits, but each mountain and stream, rock and tree has its own spirit. With all of the tides, storms, earthquakes and volcanic eruptions in Sulaweya, these were some seriously pissed off spirits. Trying to pacify them was probably the central activity of the Kelanua faith before they left the islands.

The Kelanua brought their religion with them when they came to Korvath. The spirits of this new land seemed older and sleepier – just like the slumbering elder gods of the Cthyans...

The Antorans have little use for the spirits of the Kelanua and view their religion as mere superstition. The Antorans have their own religion, after all. There were probably a variety of them back when the Antorans were divided out into their original nations, and we could easily get into all of the tribal traditions, variant sects and heretical offshoots.

Both Erica and I just love creating that kind of stuff... But it's not necessary for the game. So all we need is the main Antoran religion. It ended up fine-tuning some of our world history, too. Now it's time to get mythological!

I began with a trinity of mortals that reflect the power balance of the three Tydalus moons. I figure that there are interpretations of the religion that even consider these human figures to be mortal incarnations of the magical moons. But mostly, we're just interested in maintaining the theme set out by these satellites.

The human Grandfather figure was a Bhataari warlord named Orvo. He had united a significant portion of the steppe tribes and was gearing up to complete the job, then finish conquering the rest of Antora. His son was a great warrior and a tribal leader in his own right, a man named Rhystar. During a raid in the north, Rhystar fell in love with Zelleny, a green-eyed Strazni woman – probably with some Cthyan blood in her veins – and made her his wife. Zelleny and Rhystar became the mortal Mother and Father manifestations in the religion, which came to be known as the faith of Zelletar.

I just combined their names, but the result came out sounding pretty mystic, so I think I'll stick with it.

Zelleny the sea-eyed mother was mad – perhaps she spent too long watching the auroras, or because of her Cthyan heritage – but she was also a prophetess. She had dreams/visions that foretold the doom of Antora. She told Rhystar, who believed Zelleny and tried to convince his father to lead all the people of Antora away to safety. Warlord Orvo didn't believe a word of it, convinced that this was a Strazni trick to keep him from conquest. When Rhystar and Zelleny persisted, Orvo was furious enough to have them both tied to stakes on the plains and left them there to die.

But Rhystar and Zelleny didn't die. For seven days – or more, if I feel like I need to make this a greater magical feat – they survived without food or water, and managed not to get eaten by anything.

By the end, they were sick and tired of those mother-effing stakes on that mother-effing plain.

...Sorry, I couldn't resist.

Rhystar and Zelleny were eventually discovered and cut free by a caravan of Massir traders, who were all impressed that they had survived so long exposed to the elements. The Massir merchants believed Zelleny's story of doom, too – their own astronomers had warned that the Grandfather Moon was coming – and a band of followers began growing up around the couple.

Orvo was gathering as many of the most warlike Bhataari tribes as he could, whipping them into a frenzy of conquest and mostly ignoring his foolish son and crazed daughter-in-law. But as the ground began to tremor and Grandfather Moon loomed larger and larger in the sky, more Bhataari, Strazni and Massir flocked to Rhystar's banner. He sent messengers to beg Warlord Orvo to listen, but not one of them returned... Though Rhystar found several of them bound to stakes on the steppes. None of the messengers were as lucky or blessed as him and Zelleny.

When the quakes grew worse and the ocean began to swallow Antora, Rhystar and Zelleny led their people northwest to the land bridge. It's said that Warlord Orvo led his warriors the other way, charging into the onrushing ocean and vowing conquest – and that the sea welcomed him.

The water pursued Rhystar and Zelleny's followers all the way across Antora and the very land was falling out from under them. Rhystar and Zelleny rode at the back of the exodus to make sure that their people reached safety and no one was left behind. But then, as they were crossing the narrowest spit of stone and ice that connected Antora to Korvath, a great tidal wave came racing toward the fleeing refugees.

Zelleny and Rhystar stood hand-in-hand to face the tidal wave. And it stopped. The waters stilled until the last of their followers had crossed to higher ground. Then the wave swallowed them both, leaving the Antorans to settle the new land alone.

Zelletaran legend says that Zelleny and Rhystar will return from the ocean one day, perhaps with new visions to lead their people once more. But on that day, Orvo and his horde will ride out of the sea as well, mounted on fish-scaled steeds and armed with shark-tooth arrows.

Whew! Alright, we've got some religions. There are gods to fear and appease, some martyrs to revere, and a second coming to look forward to. One or more Antoran royal families may claim to be descendants of Rhystar and Zelleny, too.

I'm thinking that most Antorans are at least a little religious, if only because Tydalus is a dangerous world and there's no upside to angering the gods or the spirits. But the Massir in particular have studied the moons and have the math to more or less predictably plot their orbits – an erratic orbit, in the case of Grandfather Moon – so there's some room for skepticism, too.

The Kelanua's animistic religion and distrust of sea-colored eyes will certainly make them seem backward to the Antorans. After all, Zelleny had green eyes. When the Kels occasionally push green- or blue-eyed prisoners off the lighthouse, it certainly does nothing to ease tensions between them and the inlanders.

As to whether or not those sea-eyes *actually* have anything to do with manifested Cthyan genetics... Well, I'm leaving that door open for myself.

The world is built!

I know this section was a bit like trying to drink from a fire hose. I debated where to place it in the book, and wondered if I should put it *after* the story development. But the plot is very much based in the Tydalus lore and locations, so I risked positioning it up front. My fingers are crossed that it was the right decision!

It's also worth noting that this massive wall of text is *not* what I'll be handing out to my players. That would be like assigning homework before they get to play the game, and this is supposed to be fun – not information overload. I'll give my players enough to make their characters and start game, then sprinkle in the rest when they need to know it to further or understand the plot.

All of this world-building didn't happen at once. It's the result of several working dinners and long walks around the park with Erica, notes for the novel that were years old – our to-write list is *very* long – and dozens of emails we passed back and forth. I thought several times that we were done, only to hit another snag that forced me to go back and fix up some piece of Tydalus' history.

It's okay if it takes time for your game world to come together. That's normal, I promise. But that's also why it's important to only build what you need – it's already a time-consuming task to manufacture a setting and you can easily spend years on it without ever running a single game session.

Every time a new issue came up, I asked myself what the story required and how much history I needed to support it. How much information did I need to wrap my head around Tydalus and how much was just getting pointlessly into the weeds? This isn't a full game manual or world-bible for Tydalus... But it's a solid base and enough information to finally dig into the story idea rattling around my head, to set the events in places that makes sense, and fill those places with non-player characters (NPCs) that fit the setting. And to begin turning this heap of thoughts into an actual game.

So let's get started!

THE DREAM

Now that you know a bit about the world of Tydalus – alright, it was an admittedly pretty massive info-dump – my game concept might actually make some sense. It's a basic idea from right out of my ass, but we'll clean it off here and then flesh it out over the course of three increasingly detailed outlines. By the time we're finished, my players will have no idea that it began as just a random thought.

I'll keep the game story short and simple. I'm not trying to win a Hugo, just entertain my friends for a few weeks. And if the idea gets too complex, then it may become difficult for my players to follow and this book will get *way* too long.

My idea is that Tydalus is currently experiencing a historically low tide – low enough that an uncharted island has been exposed by the retreating waters. There's some kind of mysterious temple or tomb on that island, left over from the history that I detailed earlier. And then something inside wakes up and/or escapes to threaten all of Tydalus.

That's all I need to get started: low tide, temple, evil thing. Now let's turn that into a full game campaign.

THE FIRST OUTLINE

My primary outline is a basic three-point story arc. It's not always exactly three bullet points, but all we need to do right now is figure out our story's beginning, middle, and end. Knowing the ending is *key*. It gives you a destination to shoot for, and that will be important for keeping yourself on track.

My first outline for Tydalus looks like this:

1. A ship is blown off course and wrecks on an island revealed by the abnormally low tide.
2. The ship's crew discovers a temple on the island and accidentally disturbs it.
3. The horrors inside drive one of the non-player characters mad, who will have crazed but accurate insight about the monster.
4. The characters escape the mysterious island, but they must protect Korvath from what was unleashed.
5. They find magic to defeat the antagonist.
6. They deploy the magic in a final confrontation.

This is my basic map-dragon-treasure RPG outline. If you're not familiar with map-dragon-treasure, it's from *My Guide to RPG Storytelling*. But if you haven't read it or need a quick refresher, here it is:

Your game needs an antagonist. That's the dragon. Your players need to know how to reach the dragon, so you provide a map. And finally, they need incentive to go there. That's the treasure.

For Tydalus, my dragon is the monster in the temple. The map will be the non-player character that I intend to drive insane. The treasure – the incentive for my player characters – will be not dying, and keeping everyone else on Korvath from dying, too.

CHARACTERS

So now that I have the basics of my story, I need to figure out who's going to be in it. My game will require player characters (PCs, the people that my friends create and play), and non-player characters (NPCs, the people that the Storyteller creates and plays).

The PCs

This story is all about an island, which will mean getting my player characters onto a boat. The sea is something that haunts the nightmares of every human on Tydalus, so most wouldn't be caught dead on a ship. Because they would actually die.

But there are a few people that I *can* easily get onto a boat. The first ones who come to mind are the Kelanua. They watch the sea, guard the salt mines, and actually do some fishing. The Kels also have Antoran prisoners who labor in the salt mines and do a lot of the shit work of the lighthouses. I can draft them into work on a boat, too, which is arguably an even crappier job than being in the salt mines. I'm sure that my players and I can think up plenty of reasons for their characters to wind up sentenced to the coast.

And then there are Antoran mercenaries. The Kelanua population is constantly dwindling, so they need to hire additional help to deal with the dangers of the Korvath coast.

Wait, now I need to do some more world-building. The Kelanua are entirely dependent upon food sent out from the Antoran farm terraces, and don't produce anything in their lighthouses. So how could they afford to hire mercenaries?

Let me think... Well, the Kelanua have salt, right? It's important for making food taste better and preserving it to eat later. When a high tide wipes out half of the inland farms and grazing terraces, the cities need to have provisions stored up, and salt helps with that. I think we can reasonably decide that salt is important enough – and hard enough to get – to be worth its weight in gold.

So the Kelanua will pay Antoran mercenaries in salt. Now I've justified any mercenaries and expanded the world of Tydalus. Plus, I can tell my players what kind of characters to start thinking up.

The antagonists

The most important non-player character in any role-playing game is the antagonist, the evil that your players will be trying to thwart. The antagonist will shape your entire campaign, so they're worth investing some serious thought and effort into.

For Tydalus, I want the campaign enemy to be very evocative of the Cthulhu Mythos. Something horrible and ultimately unknowable, against which human weapons are useless. Now, I do need to let the player characters win in this story because if we end the world, we can't really tell any more stories in it. But I want to maintain that Lovecraftian sense of impending doom as much as I can while still keeping it fun.

I need some kind of antagonist that can be resisted, but isn't just something to fight. So I've decided on a classic Mythos monster – a shoggoth. It's a giant malevolent amoeba, pretty much an evil oil-slick with too many eyes and teeth. A shoggoth isn't something you can fight with a sword.

The characters can have other lesser monsters to actually stab and kill, and they *will* eventually defeat our ancient liquid evil, but they won't do that part with swords or bows.

One of the things that readers have requested from my guides is to see character relationships – with both allied and antagonistic

NPCs – in action. The relationship between the heroes and their foe is an important one.

And that's my first major hurdle for this particular game. Let's face it – there's not a lot of character interaction you can have with a lake of pissed-off goo.

So my story needs a secondary antagonist, someone the player characters can talk to, someone who can have more character arc than a shoggoth. I like my antagonists to be relatable. Ideally, my players will sympathize with the villain, even though they still need to stop them to save the world.

I think my secondary antagonist is going to be someone from the same ship that the game begins on. I already need the shoggoth to drive someone mad to serve as the map for my map-dragon-treasure plot. Now I have another use for them – to give the shoggoth a human face that the player characters can interact with.

I haven't quite decided who that's going to be just yet. Someone sympathetic, yes, but I'm not certain if they'll be one of the Kelanua sailors, a young mercenary, or maybe an Antoran prisoner.

That last might be the most sympathetic. Someone sentenced to the salt mines by a harsh city-state, someone whose crime was understandable, or who might even be innocent of the charges. I'll make this prisoner as likable as possible to ensure my players talk to them – and don't murder them before my story is told.

Our friendly prisoner is going to be driven mad early in the first chapter, when they encounter the shoggoth. After all, I don't want my players wandering around without their map for very long. But with the madness will come insight and wisdom, as well as an understanding of the shoggoth that can make the prisoner useful to me as the monster's human voice. This will come at a high sanity cost to the NPC, making them both a victim and the villain.

Perfect! Now this NPC is both sympathetic *and* useful.

Since a shoggoth is a difficult villain to combat with weapons, I don't want to end this game with a boss fight. So I'll use this NPC to attempt to stop the player characters from saving the day. Their thoughts are stained and their mind cracked by this incomprehensible evil, and fighting this NPC is logistically more feasible than a battle against horrible, tooth-filled slime.

But I'll be sure to give this NPC some lucid moments, too. First of all, a dribbling lunatic who operates beyond reason is a pretty trite villain. I like my antagonists to have more motivation than that. As my prisoner NPC struggles with the horrors slithering through their mind, they may welcome death. And their unique insight into evil means that they know the elder gods aren't gone. They're just sleeping and humanity is like the mice coming out at night – they don't own the house and as soon as the owners awake, they will be hunted down and exterminated. Giving the world back to the elder gods is inevitable anyway, so why let humanity suffer?

How's that for motivation? It's unhinged, certainly, but there's a method to the madness.

Finally, this is an example of the difference between an antagonist and a villain. This prisoner isn't evil, and so isn't a villain. They just don't want anyone to suffer. The NPC will provide guidance to the player characters, but in the end, they *will* work against the heroes, trying to stop them. That's the definition of an antagonist.

Other NPCs

My game will require a few other NPCs. Tydalus is a new world for my players, so I want at least one non-player character around who can help explain this world for them. I'd also like to include at least one love interest so that I can show how I build a romantic arc. But because I don't want to burden myself with too many long-term NPCs, they can be the same person.

After a little thought, I've decided to use the first mate of the ship. That would place this NPC in a position of authority over the player characters – in command of other Kelanua sailors, or giving orders to Antoran mercenaries and prisoners. I don't want to give my players a lot of orders, but I like the ability to provide direction in case the characters wander off-course or don't know what to do.

I'll make this first mate soft-spoken and thoughtful, not one to sling around a lot of orders, and make sure he serves his story role without overshadowing the player characters at all.

But I also need to ensure that the PCs go blundering into that temple early on in the story, and that doesn't sound like something this thoughtful NPC would do. So the captain of the ship will be more of a blustering old blow-hard to make sure that the horror gets unleashed. I'll remove him from the story once he's served that purpose.

For the rest of the game, I want the less hard-headed first mate in charge. He's going to be more careful and take lots of advice from the player characters. The first mate will be Kelanua – he knows the sea and the lighthouse and the salt mines, but I want the adventure to take my characters inland, into the Antoran cities. The first mate will be utterly lost in these places. After all, the Kelanua lived in the mountains, but that was many generations ago – long before he was born. If I have any Antoran characters, the first mate will defer to them on all issues concerning the mainland.

It's a simple way to keep an NPC from taking over the group and stealing the spotlight. The first mate's "orders" will involve a lot of *Hey, talk to that person for me* and *You know this place, so where should we go?* The first mate remains ostensibly in charge and I can issue some orders if I need to give the PCs a nudge, but I'll mostly have him hang back – without sacrificing his authority.

In fact, delegating tasks to the experts – my player characters – makes the first mate look smart, and makes the characters feel like experts in something. Plus, being Kelanua will make him an outcast among the Antoran majority, so that's going to put him further out of his element on the mainland, as well as creating some interesting hurdles in any potential romantic arcs.

Tydalus is a basic RPG story, so I think these are the only four non-player characters I need right now: the shoggoth, the prisoner, the captain and the first mate. I'm sure there will be some others to create along the way, but we've done enough work to get me to the next stage.

THE SECOND OUTLINE

Now it's time to turn my high-level outline into individual chapters. Each of them is designed to reveal some new part of the story or advance the game into its next act.

I'll break each chapter down into its components. Some of them will become individual scenes, and others will be lumped together. It grows pretty quickly from the first outline – as you'll see.

Chapter 1

All of the characters are on a ship... for some reason. I don't know what that reason is yet, but on the way to wherever they're going, some kind of monster will attack the boat. This accomplishes two things for me. First, the characters get something to do, and test out their combat stats. Second – and more importantly for the story – it shows how dangerous the sea is.

Writers say *show, don't tell*. That showing information you want your readers to know will always have greater impact than simply telling them. And for an RPG Storyteller, this is where we can show, not just tell.

After the monster attack, a storm brews up and the PCs will have a crisis to help crew the boat. I covered crisis scenes in both the first and second Storytelling guides, but in case you started with this book: crisis scenes are a series of skill checks or rolls to do important, exciting tasks in a role-playing game *other* than combat. Things like life-saving surgery, repairing a starfighter... or getting a ship through a storm.

One of the great things about a crisis is that you can have your player characters succeed in a story-critical challenge, no matter how badly they roll. The cost will just be high as a result. Or you can have them fail at something that they *need* to fumble, but the characters can do so gracefully if the players roll well.

In this case, no matter how well the PCs do, I need their ship to wreck on the island that's been revealed by the low tide. If they do well on their rolls, the player characters will wash ashore more or less intact. If they do poorly, they'll get beat up by the experience. But after they all pick themselves up out of the sand, the Kelanua sailors will get to work repairing the ship. Whether or not the PCs help is up to their players.

But regardless of their decision, that's when the call of Cthulhu hits. Eerie magical summons tug at the characters' minds and they must succeed in a mental crisis to resist following it. This game isn't all about physical might, and this is where the players feel it. The characters will face threats to their minds as much as their bodies. Probably more.

Any characters who fail the crisis rolls are drawn to the temple. Someone *needs* to fail for the story to progress, so even if the player characters all succeed in resisting the call, the young prisoner NPC that I described before – the one I'm going to drive over the edge and who will speak for the shoggoth – will succumb.

The ship's captain knows not to mess with anything on the sea or under it, and that means this temple. He instantly writes off the lost prisoner and says good riddance, but some old sea-dog – a wise Kelanua sailor – warns that they weren't summoned for anything good. If they don't retrieve their straggler, he says, they may regret it. So the captain reluctantly agrees that they should recapture the lost prisoner.

The player characters will be among those selected for the job, of course. I'm about ready for another combat, so I think they will encounter some creepy, hard-shelled crab-creatures along the way.

The monsters let the summoned NPC prisoner wander right past, but will attempt to stop the PCs.

Once my players fight their way through, they find the temple all made from that green-black stone that is so often mentioned in Lovecraft and Robert E. Howard's stories. The temple is both crude and graceful, but the architecture isn't designed to please human sensibilities. The NPC breaks the temple seal and enters.

I'll have the Kelanua captain or first mate lead the player characters into the temple to retrieve their lost prisoner. The unsettling building is full of murals and depictions of the stuff that I developed back in the world-building section and which will do some sanity damage to the PCs. But the temple walls seem to be covered in strange carvings of closed eyes and mouths that all look to have been made out of melted wax... But then an expendable sailor – sorry, you shouldn't have worn the red shirt today, buddy – steps on part of it and the mouth opens. Before he can scream, the mouth snaps shut, severing his leg.

A dark pseudopod drops from the ceiling and grabs a second sailor. The melting wax faces aren't carved into the walls – they're a huge creature covering the temple interior. And they've woken it up. It oozes off the walls and surges out after the characters. And the players have met our antagonist – it's evil soup.

The captain tries to hack the shoggoth in half and dies horribly for his trouble. The player characters can try to fight this fang-filled goo if they wish, but the idea is to show them that swords don't do a lot against a shoggoth. The old sea dog will tell everyone to run – and then probably die, since I really don't want anyone too knowledgeable around to provide soothing answers for the confused and hopefully frightened player characters.

There will be a crisis to escape as eye-studded pseudopods try to kill everyone. But even after they escape the temple, the PCs will have to keep running as the shoggoth oozes out after them. How big is it? Too large to easily answer that question...

I'll put in another crisis to get to the boat and get it back into the water with the shoggoth flooding inexorably toward them. This is one of those crises that I need the players to succeed, so they may take some damage or expend other resources, but I'll get them into the water and fleeing from the spreading dark stain on the horizon.

Chapter 2

The player characters sail swiftly back across the water to the lighthouse. This is the sequel.

Okay, quick break to explain some terminology here. In writing, authors often talk about the scene/sequel breakdown. A "scene" is where stuff happens, when there's action or knowledge dumps, and events occur. If a novel is made up of only action-packed scenes, the narrative becomes both exhausting and difficult to follow.

Readers require an occasional break to absorb what happened, and so do the characters in the novel – that's the sequel. A scene's sequel is a rest, the pause between waves. It helps break the story into digestible chunks, and does the same for a role-playing game. It gives your characters and your players a moment to breathe, to understand and discuss what just happened and then what to do next. You *can* run two or more scenes back-to-back and it will create a great sense of momentum, but be careful how often you do it. Too much can exhaust your player group.

It's still early in the game and I don't want to ramp things up like that yet, so I'll give my player characters a moment to rest and react to what happened on the island. But the huge shoggoth is following at a distance as they return to the lighthouse.

The Keeper of the Tower – which is the title that I've given the commander of a Kelanua lighthouse – will want to talk to the first mate, since he's the highest-ranked survivor of the island temple. I'll let the player characters have their say, too, and warn whoever they wish about the monster that followed them out of the temple, or ask any questions of the prisoner who woke the shoggoth. They won't have much to say just yet, though.

The Keeper of the Tower believes the PCs story and turns on the lighthouse's warning lamp. I'm not quite sure yet if that is a light pattern or a different colored reflector, but it's something that only happens at high tide. The warning light has never been lit at low tide before. Oh, shit.

Hopefully that will demonstrate how bad this is.

The other Kelanua lighthouses will send help, but that will take time. The shoggoth is still sludging toward land, though, and until those reinforcements arrive, the PCs will need to help hold the fort. Literally...

Besieging the lighthouse will be a protracted action scene, so I think I'll break it down into an alternating sequence of two fights and two crises.

The dark, evil goop unleashed from the temple has stopped at a distance from the lighthouse, but that doesn't mean it has given up. The shoggoth will call up all sorts of horrors from the deep ocean. Crab-men march on the lighthouse and scuttle up the huge tower, trying to get in. So my first fight takes place on a balcony. Not much happening with the terrain except a deathly plummet on at least one side. I should make this fight simple and fairly low difficulty. After all, the PCs have more action coming up.

The crab-things continue scaling the tower, but I don't want just another combat, so this one will be a crisis instead. This time, the crab-monsters are scaling a side of the tower with no balconies or something. The PCs will need to rappel down the lighthouse on ropes, fighting while swinging around and sweeping crab-men off the lighthouse. NPCs may fall and need to be caught, player characters might risk their own plunge, and they can swing to new areas.

I don't want the players getting bored with one combat after another, so I hope this will keep the tension high in a more entertaining way while still inflicting some damage on their characters.

Finally, the PCs get hauled back up the lighthouse and I can give them a short sequel here. Not for long, but time enough to catch their breath and trade a few words. NPCs – especially the first mate – can wonder what the shoggoth is thinking, or if it thinks at all. Maybe the maddened prisoner NPC can begin talking about the strange ancient magic that I'll use to send them on their adventure.

But before the PCs can get into any prolonged conversation, a bell rings. It's an alarm – something has breached the lighthouse.

Crab-monsters have broken into the tower and the PCs rush off to deal with them. The fight is harder this time, with a more difficult venue – though I'm not sure what that is yet. I'll figure it out in the next phase. The characters are a little beat up now, and I can increase the number of enemies on the map to ramp things up.

From there, I can roll right into the next event or give the PCs another sequel, depending on what I think they need. Remember that the goal here is *not* to beat your players.

Honestly, that's a shitty game because the Storyteller can *always* win. I get to decide how strong the enemies are, how many to throw at the PCs, how many times to attack them, and I can lie about my dice rolls. If I want to, I'll win. Easily. But if I do, then my story ends too soon. The player characters all die and the world of Tydalus drowns in malevolent goop – and it's not even high tide. That's not a very satisfying story and my players are going to be understandably pissed that I pulled that stunt.

Role-playing isn't me against my players. My job as Storyteller is to entertain and maybe challenge them. Their characters are the heroes of my story, so my job is to give them opportunities to be heroic. If the characters can't handle another crisis or fight, I'll give my players a break. But I'm confident they'll be up to the challenge.

Now it's time for the vast shoggoth to fill the horizon and give the player characters a horrifying eyeful – and probably take some sanity damage. The monstrous stain is the size of a lake and begins undergoing some kind of mitosis, with amoebas splitting off and swarming the lighthouse. It's time for another crisis, this time to use siege weapons and pour boiling tar down the sides of the tower.

Just one of the shoggoth amoebas makes it through to the lighthouse and the characters will have to fight it. I've gone past the two fights I initially imagined, but this is the last one and I think it will work because it's a small-scale indicator and reminder of what they face with the full-sized shoggoth.

This is the hardest fight of the chapter. The shoggoth amoeba is a liquid, so swords, arrows and harpoons just splash through. It's like your soup is trying to kill you. How do you fight against that? With paper towels? Umm… that's a good question. I have to let my characters fight the evil goop without destroying it. I want to send them off to find some ancient magic, but that doesn't work if they can just kill the shoggoth.

I think that I'll use fire here. Most animals fear fire and shy away from flames. It's kept humans safe for eons, and there's some primal satisfaction in that. I can make sure that they get some pitch and a torch, then let them coat their weapons with burning tar or light their arrows on fire. That will force the bit of shoggoth into retreat, but they still can't kill it.

The PCs have been fighting all day. Or maybe for multiple days, depending on what kind of sequels I needed to give them. Either way is fine – the shoggoth keeps on coming. There's nothing left to do… The lighthouse has used all of their resources to fight, and now the Kelanua are out of pitch and oil.

But just when all hope seems lost, ships appear from the north. It's the reinforcements from another lighthouse, and the sailors onboard begin firebombing the shoggoth, which retreats back from the flames. Pitch and oil burn on water, so the Kelanua can create a sort of flaming barrier that holds it back.

The shoggoth is thwarted… temporarily. But it's low tide, so the Kelanua lighthouses weren't exactly ready for an attack and their stocks are low. They can hold it back, but not forever.

The player characters are nominated to find some way to drive the shoggoth away, banish it, or put it back to sleep before supplies run out and the monster spreads across all of Korvath.

Chapter 3

In the last chapter, the maddened prisoner NPC mentioned some kind of ancient magic that can deal with the shoggoth. It's not much to go on, but no one has any better ideas about how to banish the monster, so the Kelanua send the player characters up to another lighthouse – the first of their lighthouses, where the oldest keepers live and the location of their largest library – to learn more.

The most direct route is by sea, so they are sent up along the coast. Well, the captain of the ship they were using is now dead, so guess who gets a promotion? The first mate remains in command of the mission and this is a lighthouse matter, so his control is still firm. But there's also not a lot of decisions to make right now, so there's not much that he needs to tell the PCs to do. Good – they're the heroes of this story, not my first mate turned captain.

This journey to the old Kelanua lighthouse is another chance for a sequel. A lot has happened in a short period, and the characters may need some time to talk, ask questions and get to know their important NPCs. Their new captain probably has a healthy respect for them based on their heroism on the island and at the lighthouse, so he'll be open to dialog.

My players can also talk to the prisoner NPC. They should be mostly lucid at this point so that we have room for them to get more unhinged. If I have them go totally nuts now, I can't ramp it up later – and I want to show a slow slide into Lovecraft-style insanity. The PCs can discuss and learn a bit about what's going on, but shouldn't discover too many details right now.

During the voyage, the ship is attacked again. Maybe crab-men, or maybe something else. I'm not sure yet and I'll take a look at how many of those crab-monsters I've had them fight at this point. If it's a lot, then I will find something else terrifying to pick a fight with a ship.

Was the monster sent after them by the shoggoth? Is that malevolent sludge even intelligent enough to know what the characters are up to? No one knows – and it doesn't matter – but I can keep my players wondering and hopefully start getting them a little paranoid. This is a cosmic horror game, after all.

The characters finally reach the oldest Kelanua lighthouse and are told or otherwise find out about the power that can save them all – an Elder Sign. It's located in some lost inland shrine, known to the Kelanua as a place that the ancient Cthyans shunned. If it was bad for those who worshiped the elder gods, then it's probably good for humanity.

Long ago, the Kelanua searched for the Elder Sign in hopes of using it as a weapon against the Cthyans or for protection during high tide, but they always failed to find it. Or failed to return at all.

This whole endeavor might be a wild gull chase. (Hmm, is it too heavy-handed to adapt that phrase to a sea bird more appropriate for Tydalus?) But swords aren't going to stop that thing, so they have to try to find this Elder Sign.

The PCs head inland, into the mountains of Korvath. The NPC captain is still in charge, but now they're leaving his area of expertise behind and he'll wisely let those more familiar with this land and their customs take the lead. This man listens well – he listened to the old sea dog in Chapter I, he'll listen to the PCs, and respect their thoughts. He can still speak up if the players don't know what to do or get stuck, or if it looks like my game is going off the rails.

But wherever possible, your players should do the talking and devise the plans. Whenever the NPC captain makes a call or gives an order, he will just be repeating whatever it was that the players said or recommended. Don't worry, they will still argue about going east or west for twenty minutes before deciding on west, so when an NPC boils their conversation down into a single line and gives the order to head west, they will sound authoritative – even though your players actually made the call.

Now the story of Tydalus gets some inland travel time, a sequel after our research field trip and info-dump session, providing my players more time to interact with each other and with the NPCs.

Let's take a moment to talk about the Elder Sign that my player group is after. What is it, precisely? It originates from the Cthulhu Mythos, but within the context of Tydalus... I'm not sure yet. It's probably some kind of magic from beyond the stars or from when humanity was still just protein slime not even dreaming about becoming single-celled organisms. It's magic that human minds can hardly fathom, so explaining where it comes from or how it works doesn't really make sense. As long as it functions in our story and has internal consistency, we're good.

In case you're not familiar with the Elder Sign from Lovecraft's Mythos, it's basically a wobbly pentagram with an eye drawn in the middle. It's a magic scribble. Why can't my characters just draw one on their foreheads and be immune to giant toothy amoeba death? Why aren't the lighthouses covered in Elder Sign graffiti?

Well, when you use magic in any game or story, you get to play the magic card. Magic has whatever rules you give it. And as long as you are firm and consistent about what those rules are, they work. *My* Elder Sign was inscribed with arcane arts now lost to Tydalus and perhaps never known to humans.

So suck it. My characters get *one* special doodle and they better not lose it or screw it up because they can't inscribe a new one.

Okay, we figured out the nature of the magical weapon, and why it's so special. The players shouldn't be able to poke too many plot holes in it, so let's move on.

The PCs head to a place the Cthyans supposedly avoided when they were around and where most of the Kelanua searched. There are no signs of any ancient temples, hidden valleys, or mystic caves, but there is a small town. The characters might as well restock their supplies and sleep in some beds. And maybe the people here have some helpful local legends.

The NPC captain will make the player characters do most of the talking here – remember, the Kels are a minority ethnic group that don't deal with the Antorans very much. He doesn't know inlander customs, and people here will be strange to him. So the captain will turn to the other characters.

The town in question is a quaint little mountain village with a nice church. And if you've read any Lovecraft, then you know this is a bad sign. The villagers will answer any questions put to them, and be more or less hospitable, but they don't seem to know anything about any ancient secrets, magic signs, or mighty weapons. At the church, the priest is a bit more mysterious, but also plays innocent.

Frustrated, the NPC captain will recommend that they move on in the morning. For all they know, the secret place could have been buried in a quake or avalanche centuries ago.

But that night, the villagers attempt to murder the PCs in their beds. Big surprise. The characters might be able to fight off the first wave, but the entire town has been mobilized against them in a religious fervor. Every last man, woman, and child has a knife or sharp stick and the intention to stab it into one of the outsiders.

The PCs are likely better trained and better armed, but they're outnumbered a hundred to one. The NPC captain will shout to run and will book it himself. If I've generated some rapport between him and the player characters – or if they obey his orders – they'll follow. Otherwise, I'll throw a few waves of armed villagers at the PCs, then make it obvious there's always another one coming.

Staying here to fight means staying to die, but don't just *say* that! Players get cranky and stubborn if you tell them that they can't win. Which makes sense – who plays an RPG to lose? But I can make them *want* to leave, and the NPC captain can remind the characters that they're here to find the Elder Sign, not to kill angry villagers.

Next will come the crisis to run away. Rooftop jumping, hiding from search parties, stuff like that. But the insane NPC falls behind and gets captured. The player characters can see them being taken into the church. By now, the players surely know that things aren't what they seem here. Maybe the Elder Sign is in this town after all – and if it is, it's probably in the church.

From a safe distance, the characters can plan their break-in. I'll prepare a couple of options: if the PCs go in by stealth, if they try to infiltrate disguised as villagers, or if they charge in right through the front door with swords swinging.

Can my players think up another way to get inside the church? Probably. But chances are good that I can steal rolls and steps from the scenes that I *did* prepare to make it work. Worst case scenario, I'll wing it. I can't expect players to stick to my outline every session. As long as they're going into the church, then they're moving the story in the right direction. I only have a problem if they decide to wander off and ignore the quest entirely. And if they do that, then we have a much bigger problem than my notes.

I think that I'll protect the church with magical wards or locks. Magic's hard on the soul and using it is a good way to lose your mind, but the villagers are already unhinged. The player characters have to get through mystic wards – which is a new challenge – and they have to deal with some sanity damage to do it.

Inside the church will be murals similar to those in the temple on the island back at the beginning. I can flesh out some backstory if I still need to drop any information, or if I need to remind my players about anything.

But just looking at these profane and blasphemous images is disturbing. Here's where we throw some awareness or investigation skill checks to see if they notice things – and the players beg to skip the rolls because by now, they all know better than to look. There's information to learn... but if ignorance is bliss, then knowledge is madness.

Important backstory to drop here – the priests of this little town guard the Elder Sign. But not to keep it safe. They protect the Sign to prevent anyone from using it against their elder god masters. They can't destroy it, but they *can* keep the thing locked up. Some fanatical cultists can always monologue about it if I need them to.

The goal in this scene is to rescue the prisoner NPC – probably saving them from sacrifice to the elder gods or something – and then get the Elder Sign. I may put the sign in a book, since the characters won't know how to use it. An instruction manual of sorts... But maybe not. This might be a good place for the mad prisoner to really show their use and repay all of the effort that has gone into keeping them safe by being able to give those instructions.

I can figure out those details later. Right now, they'll only slow me down.

Next, the player characters need to escape the church with the Elder Sign and their mad friend. There were probably some combats involved in getting them, so I'll use a crisis for the getaway.

Chapter 4

I could stretch this out into a dozen chapters if I wanted to get more intricate, but for the purposes of this book, I'll keep things simple. So now it's time to wrap things up.

This is the climax of the story and I want to keep tensions high. The characters just escaped the creepy mountain village, but they didn't kill everyone there, so those enemies can still make things hard for the outsiders. I'll have them summon something nasty to chase the party, maybe a Hound of Tindalos or night-gaunt – both classic Mythos monsters.

I could do this one as a fight or a crisis. Not sure yet which, but I'm leaning toward a combat. I'll pin it down in the final outline.

After dealing with the pursuing monster, the player character group will need to cover some ground to make it back to their ship.

In order to keep things moving quickly this close to the end, I think I'll put that monster attack partway through the journey back so I can just segue to it after I narrate the summoning.

After that, I'll finally allow the characters some sequel time to figure out how they use the Elder Sign. Do they just wave it at the shoggoth until it goes away? Trying to answer that question – either reading a book or asking the prisoner NPC – will give the players something to do on their way back to the lighthouse.

As they get closer, I'll give them the answer: the Elder Sign must be taken to the island temple, the origin of the evil. Returning to the temple gives my game a certain amount of symmetry as they go back to where this all began. I'm also reversing the first chapter's conflict, where they fought to escape the temple.

But the worse news is that the Elder Sign requires the sacrifice of a willing human life to make it work. Cue dramatic music!

So now the characters need to return to the island, but the shoggoth is in their way. The Kelanua ships have managed to keep it from making landfall, but the temple island is on the other side of the evil oil-slick.

The player characters can attempt to sail around the shoggoth, but it reacts and tries to bar their way. The Elder Sign repels the monster, though, so they can sail to the island. But it's not powered by a human life yet and they're not at the temple, so it's not much of a reprieve. Strange storms toss the ship and the shoggoth itself gives chase, indirectly attacking with huge waves and eating away at the characters' fraying sanity with its gibbering.

When they finally land on the shores of the island, the shoggoth follows. There's a scramble to get off the ship before the monster destroys it, and the shoggoth surges over the whole thing as soon as everyone is away. It still can't get close enough to attack, even as it flows over the rest of the island.

The crab-monsters make their final appearance to try to stop the player group. My characters have fought them before, and now the PCs get to test their new and improved power level against this old enemy. And hopefully feel good about how much stronger they are now.

The shoggoth and/or crab-monsters can kill off any minor NPCs from the ship, highlighting the danger. But the PCs finally arrive at the ancient temple and without the shoggoth covering the walls, they can see the obscene frescoes and statuary that were obscured before. They will take some more sanity damage and I'll hint that this temple is dedicated to some greater evil, something larger and even more unfathomable. The shoggoth is just the scum on the surface of the pond, hiding the horrors that lurk in the depths.

I like that. I may use that description in the final notes.

The characters are set to charge up the Elder Sign by sacrificing one of their own when the maddened prisoner makes their move. They try to disrupt the ritual or maybe destroy the Elder Sign. I can do that with a short crisis. I want to give my players a chance to talk their friend out of it rather than just kill the poor prisoner.

With the mad NPC dead or dealt with, it's time to make the final sacrifice. I'll give all of my player characters the chance to volunteer, but I'll make sure one of the NPCs survives to step in if none of the players want to give up their characters.

Which they sometimes don't. The players have spent the whole campaign trying to keep their characters alive and even in a game this short they can get attached. I'll also be cautious if anyone has become romantically involved with any of the NPCs. I tend not to kill love interests very often because players can become just as invested in them as their own characters.

Even non-romantically entangled NPCs can sometimes have a profound effect on the group when you kill them. I once saddled a group with a damaged AI that had a child-like understanding and when it sacrificed itself for them, all of my players cried.

So I may be able to sacrifice the NPC captain here, but there's a more dramatic option. If my player characters talked the prisoner off the ledge instead of killing them, they will be ready to repay that kindness. The prisoner knows better than anyone about the horrors from beyond human perception, and might be willing to sacrifice their life to save all of humanity. For a little while, at least.

But I really hope one of the player characters is willing to make the sacrifice. I want them to remain in the spotlight and maintain the most agency in my story. We'll see how it goes.

The shoggoth oozes all around the old temple, rearing up like a tidal wave to swamp the building. But as the sacrifice dies – I don't think the method of death matters, only that it's a willing death – the Elder Sign scorches the monster away.

With that, the player characters finally win. As much as anyone wins in the Cthulhu Mythos. There are still horrors lurking beyond the stars and beneath the sea, just waiting to devour humanity. But for now, Tydalus is safe.

After that, I just need to wrap things up. Now that the shoggoth is gone, Kelanua ships arrive at the island and give the remaining characters a lift. They can just sail away, but I hope that leaving the temple standing will creep them out. If the players want, they can tell the ships to bombard the temple and try to collapse it, ensuring that the inner chambers are never opened, and pray the tide never reveals it again.

Back at the lighthouse, any mercenary characters are paid their wages in salt – along with a hefty bonus. Any prisoners are granted their freedom and all of the PCs are offered homes here in the lighthouse. They've earned respect and acceptance from the Kelanua.

If anyone has engaged in a romantic relationship with the NPC Kelanua captain, they might stay. Or if he sacrificed himself, maybe one of them will take his place. Other PCs may run off as fast as they can, swearing never to come within sight of the sea again. Or perhaps they will make the more heroic choice and stand with the Kelanua in their vigil against the ocean.

The end!

THE DICE
(AKA THE THIRD OUTLINE)

Now it's time for me to write up the final campaign outline. These are the notes that I'll use to actually run my game, so you'll see the notes I leave for myself, descriptions that I want to remember, and crises and combat stats.

Because I don't own any RPG systems and haven't invented my own, I can't use any specific rules. So I'll have to be a little circumspect when it comes to actual rolls and stats. This isn't a module, after all – it's just an example of how I put my games together. You can run this story for your group if you want, but you'll have to do a little legwork to fill in the rules.

I don't have character concepts or stats for the PCs yet, so there will be some blank spots until we go through character creation. But I'll cover my bases for any Antoran prisoner characters, mercenaries, or Kelanua crew as best I can.

And as we go, I'll place notes inside brackets *[like this]* to explain how and why I create this final outline the way that I do.

Here we go!

CHAPTER 1

Low Tide

[I name each scene or section in my game notes. I don't remember when I started doing it, but it helps me remember at a glance what I'm supposed to be doing. I check the name and sometimes that's enough for me to run the next scene. Sometimes I make the section names funny, but I'm not really sure why – I'm the only one who sees them.]

Grandfather Moon is far from Tydalus and the tide is low. The lowest in many years... The superstitious of Korvath believe that it's a good sign and represents rising fortunes. Several of the Antoran city-states are considering some new farming terraces further down their mountains. Even when the Father and Mother Moons bring in the little tides, their watermarks lie far below the last salt-encrusted line.

For the Kelanua living on the west coast, the extraordinarily low tide means that the city-states pay less attention to them than ever. During high tide, the great lighthouses are the first line of defense... But while Grandfather Moon is away, they are simply a burden. The stipends and shipments sent out by the Antoran cities come late or short of promised amounts.

But the Kels are all too used to being overlooked by the inlanders. They have always found a way to survive before, and they are determined to do so again. Fishing boats set out from each of the lighthouses to harvest food from the sea. Kelanua sailors crew the boats, but Antoran prisoners from the salt mines are often brought along to row when the winds aren't favorable.

Other Antorans on the ships don't wear chains. High tide or low, the dark seas of Tydalus are always dangerous. Even though no one knows the oceans or how to fight what lives in them better than the Kelanua, their numbers dwindle with every generation and they must hire any inlander mercenaries willing to set foot on a boat.

[That's all scene-setting, mostly for myself. When game starts, I'll probably recite this or something like it to my players, but I usually don't read the notes out verbatim.]

The Kelanua ship *Iron Eel* has been ordered out to sea to bring back fish to the people of the lighthouse known as The Hunter. *[It's time to get specific with the lighthouses, and I've decided to name them each after the Kelanua constellation found most directly overhead. So I had to make up some constellations.]*

The *Iron Eel* rides the low waves and the Antoran prisoners on the oars look out to sea anxiously. Most of them had never seen the ocean until sentenced to the salt mines along Korvath's coast. And they're not excited about this new job on the water.

While most Antorans don't believe in wild Kel tales of monsters and magic, they know that the sea is... well, if not actually evil, then at least *wrong*. Antoran history is tainted by their own bad relationship with the ocean and no rational person sets foot in seawater. But here they are...

Even the armed inlander mercenaries are nervous, though they show it less. They have seen the horrors of war, at least, and believe themselves ready for the horrors of the open sea.

Captain Nakhona strides across the deck of the *Iron Eel*, a salt-crusted cloak billowing out behind him in the stiff wind, and approaches the mercenaries – who happen to be standing near any player characters who are prisoners and bringing along with him any who might be Kelanua. Nakhona warns the mercenaries that they're outside the range of The Hunter's weapons now. Until they dock safely again, they had all better keep their eyes open and their swords ready. It's time to earn their salt.

When the captain leaves, a young prisoner nervously addresses the characters. She's an Antoran girl of mostly Strazni blood, with light hair and blue eyes. Her name is Danya and she's a prisoner of the lighthouse, sentenced to work the salt mines there. She's thin and has a racking cough from the mines, but Danya's curious about the mercenaries. As a younger girl, she wanted to become a merc. The life of a wandering blade-for-hire seemed glamorous, exciting and a rare opportunity to see the world. Danya always wanted to see the thirteen peaks – the thirteen tallest mountains on Korvath and the homes of the Antoran city-states.

Danya will hesitantly ask for some stories from the mercenaries – or from the Kelanua, if anybody is playing one. If the characters have any questions for Danya, she will remain shy, but willing to talk about herself.

Danya grew up in Athol, a village on the slopes of Vanhome. *[I didn't actually name either of these places until forced to in Chapter 3, so I had to backtrack and place the names here.]* Danya had no money and no way to get the training she needed to become a mercenary like she dreamed, and none of the soldiers would teach such a scrawny little girl.

Their loss... Danya's a fighter, as the city watch discovered when a gang of boys cornered and tried to rape her. She stabbed two of them and the rest ran away. But when one of the boys died from the wound, Danya was charged with murder and sent to the coast.

[It's a tragic and sympathetic backstory. Danya is the NPC that I've decided to send to the temple to wake the shoggoth and lose her mind. I need my players to like and understand Danya, so I gave her a background that would incline them to side with her against what are going to be mounting difficulties. Plus, I'll need Danya to give them a lot of information later, so it's best if I set the precedent now that she's talkative and willing to share stories.]

Attacked at Sea

The oldest Kelanua sailor – a bent, wrinkled, and gray man named Hoka – limps toward the mercenaries. *[I stopped referring to him in my notes as a "sea dog," because the Kelanua never domesticated wolves. That was the Antorans, while the Kels prefer cats domesticated from the native Korvath mountain lions.]*

Something is coming, Hoka says, and he can feel a storm in his aching bones. And something worse aching in his mind. *[I'm establishing a sort of intuition for evil that feels appropriate to Tydalus, and I'll need it later for Danya as she becomes a source of information.]* Captain Nakhona scoffs at the older Kel, but his young first mate, Alak'ai (or Alak for short) listens. He asks the other man if he's certain, then shouts for sailors to get to battle stations.

The old ship hand is proved correct as something huge swells the waters beneath the *Iron Eel*, then breaks the surface violently. Tentacles whip out of the water, thrashing and searching out living bodies. The ropey lengths of flesh are studded in unblinking fish-like eyes and within seconds two crew – a Kelanua sailor and an inlander prisoner – are snatched from the deck and dragged under the churning water.

Combat map: Sea, ship deck.

[This note tells me which map to bring up in case I freeze and forget. I use a digital mapping program that lets me draw or place art, which players can see in real time. I get to be pretty creative and my players can display the map on their own laptops instead of having to sit around a table with map tiles or miniatures that my cats might run off with.]

Sanity damage: The creature attacking the *Iron Eel* is more than a giant squid. A normal squid – no matter how giant – doesn't have eyes on their tentacles, and human minds shrink from the sight of this monster.

Each player character has to resist some low sanity damage at the sight of the tentacles. *[If you want to run this game for yourself, you'll need to come up with something compatible with whatever system you're using – some adaptation of healing surges, hit points, willpower, energy, or whatever.]*

And that's just the tentacles. The bulk of the creature is still underwater below the ship, but with a mental stat + alertness skill, the PCs can see the twisted shape of its body... And suffer another small dose of sanity damage. *[Here's where my players start cringing every time I give them an alertness-style check. The sense of paranoia it creates is perfect for a cosmic horror game.]*

NPC bonuses: Kelanua sailors charge into battle – including the captain – but Alak'ai fights at the PCs' side. Alak provides a bonus attack to one character each round.

[This is an example of an NPC bonus, which I detailed in the first two Storytelling guides. It's a bonus that a non-player character provides to assist the PCs. An extra attack is pretty much the best thing that the characters can have in a fight, so it's a good bonus for an NPC I want the players to like. I'll describe Alak hacking through tentacles and carrying his own weight, but I don't make any dice rolls for him and he deals no damage to the tentacles on the map. The bonus Alak'ai gives is something for the players to use. The players can decide who gets Alak's NPC bonus each round, giving them a resource to use tactically.]

Special rules: *[This section is where I'll outline any special modifications for the opponents, the terrain, or some other bad thing that will happen during the fight. Oh wait, I have an idea for one...]*

During the second round of combat, Danya gets grabbed by a tentacle and is yanked toward the deck railing. If the PCs can inflict X amount of damage *[depending on what system you use]*, then the tentacle releases her. Alternately, a physical stat + brawl or athletic skill roll can pry Danya free. *[Having to rescue Danya now will start the ball rolling on protecting her and also give the players something to do besides just make an attack during this fight.]*

Tentacle stats: Each tentacle is treated as an individual enemy and there are two for each player. All of the eye-covered tentacles will need to be defeated before the monster slinks back down into the depths.

[And this is where I would normally write down all of the enemy's specific attacks and bonuses, but we've talked several times about the legal issues involved. I can, however, discuss how *I make combat stats.]*

This is the very first fight of Tydalus. Now's not the time to kick my PCs' asses. This is their first battle and their combat skills are new, so this is to let them get used to their abilities.

I'm giving the tentacles low health and nothing special damage-wise. They will have a grappling attack, though, that may require the PCs to help each other get free – or they can have Alak use his NPC bonus to automatically get someone out.

Another kind of attack will sweep across the ship's deck to hit multiple PCs. I try to give each enemy at least two types of attacks so they don't hit repeatedly with the same one. That's boring.

I can also have the tentacles attack in groups to take advantage of a group-attack mechanic in this system that either grants a bonus to damage or to hit. If the PCs cut through the tentacles too quickly, more can always pop out of the water. This is a monster – there are no rules for how many tentacles it has.

Riders on the Storm

[I guess I got bored just naming each scene literally, so now I'm going to start mixing in song titles. Apparently.]

Now the characters have seen first-hand how dangerous the sea can be. Hoka can't name the monstrosity that attacked the ship, but the old Kelanua can certainly tell them that it's not the worst thing to spawn in the depths. During high tide, such creatures swim inland to hunt around the foothills of the drowning mountains. And the horrors that make that eye-covered squid seem frail rise from the abyss to lord over the seas. Maybe the monsters that swim inland are only fleeing those elder nightmares...

The *Iron Eel* deploys its nets and begins the job they came to do – bring back a hold full of fish to restock the dwindling stores of The Hunter. Kelanua sailors work the nets while the Antoran mercenaries warily watch the sea for trouble.

Danya will take a liking to any of the characters who saved her. She will continually pester them for stories and thank them for her life. Captain Nakhona always yells at her to get back to work, but she's as attached to the player group as a puppy.

By the end of that first day, the shore vanishes behind the *Iron Eel*, though the tall spear-shape of The Hunter thrusts thousands of feet into the air, shining its light out in a reassuring arc. But at the end of the second day, even the great lighthouse disappears below the horizon and tensions on the ship mount even higher.

That second evening, the sky takes on an unhealthy green cast as the sun sets. Hoka limps over to Captain Nakhona and cautions that the weather is about to change. Nakhona scans the cloudless sky and dismisses Hoka's warning, muttering that this will be his last voyage – the old man is obviously no longer fit for such duty and should probably be retired to lampkeeping or something within the lighthouse.

Alak'ai looks like he wants to argue with Nakhona, but the first mate just shakes his head. He walks the deck, checking and making sure that everything is tied down, if not storm-ready.

Hoka is right. *[Of course he is. I'm not just playing to the wise old sailor archetype, but I want the characters listening to Hoka's wisdom and advice on the island when we get there.]* The dark night hides the strange greenish tint to the sky, but when it's time for the Mother and Father Moons to rise, they're hidden by thick, dark clouds that cover the western horizon.

The ocean surges and strong winds churn the inky surface into waves. Captain Nakhona calls for all hands to get on deck, shouting to be heard over the swiftly growing storm. A wave sweeps one of the sailors overboard and snaps the rigging. Sails and ropes thrash in the wind. A yard-arm swings and brains another sailor. With the losses in the attack, there are too few able-bodied sailors to get the ship safely through the storm.

[It's crisis time! I'll start off explaining the storm build-up, then let the players know the first thing that goes wrong. During a crisis scene, give your PCs a chance to direct their own reactions to the events, then fit their ideas to the roll in your notes or change the roll to fit it. If no one has any ideas, then you can announce the roll(s) required to help in the crisis. It's always better to let the players have their own ideas before the Storyteller offers up the scripted ones.]

The storm is rough. Each of the PCs must make a physical stat + athletics, dodge, or boating skill check as barrels tumble across the deck, snapped hawsers whip through the air, and the pitching deck tries to shake everyone off their feet.

On a successful roll, the character takes no damage. If they fail, then the PC takes X amount of health damage. *[I'll keep the hits small here because this isn't one of our big, scary crises. I just want to bruise the characters a little.]*

The *Iron Eel* rocks violently and another sailor goes overboard. Alak'ai shouts and grabs them as they fly over the rail, struggling to haul them back onto the deck. Behind him, the yard-arm swings again. It'll hit him in the back, sending Alak and the sailor both overboard. Helping them will require rolling an appropriate physical stat + athletics, or maybe a brawl skill.

[I was deliberately non-specific above about how the player characters might save Alak. They can grab the yard-arm's ropes and heave it back, or they could tackle Alak out of the way. Or they may come up with something I haven't thought of. It probably doesn't change the roll much, so it doesn't matter and the players should be encouraged to be creative. Maybe they'll just shout a warning to Alak and I can change the roll to a social stat + social skill to warn him in time to duck.]

The players must succeed by X to save Alak'ai. This is a group roll, meaning the player characters may work together or combine individual efforts – one PC can tackle Alak while two others pull on the yard-arm's ropes – but success on their rolls get added together to save the endangered NPC.

If the PCs succeed, then Alak'ai and the sailor remain onboard the *Iron Eel*. Hooray!

But on a failed check, Alak'ai goes overboard. The sailor that he saved gets sucked under the swirling water, but Alak'ai swims well and didn't get hit in the head by a yard-arm. There's time to rescue the first mate, but he will get swamped eventually or the ship will drift away in the storm.

If any players critically failed on their roll *[a natural 1, botch or boxcars, depending upon your gaming system]*, then they go over with Alak'ai, too, and will require rescue.

Someone needs to get Alak – and potentially one of the PCs – back onto the ship. *[This is a crisis sub-stage, a section that is only triggered by failure on a roll.]*

It will require a physical stat + athletics skill to throw a rope into the water and haul up their lost crew. If a PC went over, too, then they can help with a physical stat + athletics, swimming or perhaps boating roll. It takes X amount of success to get Alak'ai back from the sea. This is a group check.

If this roll fails, the characters get Alak'ai back onto the *Iron Eel*, but the storm batters everyone as they struggle and they each take X amount of damage. *[I'll make this a larger dose of damage, since it's the result of several sequentially failed checks and should have steeper consequences as a result.]*

[But notice that the characters will retrieve Alak'ai even if they failed the dice rolls – the cost will simply be higher. Alak is a part of the story I'm telling, so I need him to live. But this doesn't mean that the characters can never fail... It's important that my players never know whether the cost of failure on a crisis roll is just going to be taking some damage while hauling Alak'ai out of the water, or if he will drown. Keeping my players guessing when it's "safe" to fail a roll

and when it's not is a very *important part of making the crisis system work.]*

Alak is grateful and will tell the PCs so later – but right now, there's no time. The storm is still tossing the *Iron Eel* around like a leaf in a turbulent stream. The yard-arm sweeps across the deck again and everyone throws themselves flat. Alak shouts for someone to get up in the rigging and tie the damned thing down! It will be a physical stat + athletics, climbing or boating skill to scramble up and help old Hoka – past his prime, my ass – to secure the arm.

The players need X amount of success. Each character who fails contributes nothing to the total, then also falls from the rigging, taking X amount of damage in the landing.

[This crisis is mostly physical attributes with athletics and boating as the main skills. If one of the characters uses a social stat/skill combo to warn Alak'ai, then that gives us some more variety, which is nice. But there's not much I can do in a boating crisis to employ many other skills. So long as the crisis doesn't go on too long, it should be okay, though. And, as always, encourage your players to be creative. If someone can think up a way to use their basket-weaving skill to tie off the rigging or pull someone out of the sea, then let them roll it. If I have any Kelanua characters in my group, then they'll probably have boating, swimming, and knot-tying skills that they'll get to use. Characters like that can carry the group in a crisis – but don't worry, the other players will have their chance to shine later.]

Shipwrecked

The *Iron Eel* is battered by the storm, pushed by racing winds and surging currents. Heavy rain falls in thick sheets, reducing visibility to nothing. The lookout shouts a warning and the ship lurches beneath everyone's feet...

And the characters wake battered and bruised in the first light of morning on a beach covered in sharp, barnacle-encrusted stones.

Being shipwrecked and spending the night on rocks with the cold sea trying to drag them back in is *not* restful. The PCs haven't recovered at all and don't get any natural healing after the storm.

Everyone picks themselves up and takes stock. The *Iron Eel* is grounded on the rocky shore. The hull is damaged and the ship is in bad shape, but her spine isn't broken and both the keel and mast remain intact. That means that the ship can sail again... with a few repairs.

Captain Nakhona, Alak'ai, Hoka, and Danya have survived the shipwreck *[all of the people I need for my story]*, as well as a significant portion of the crew and prisoners. Nakhona begins shouting for the crew to secure the *Iron Eel* before the waves drag it off the rocks and sink it for good. They need the ship beached until repairs are made.

But where the hell are they...? There are no charted islands in this area. The rocks are jagged and covered in barnacles, anemones, and strands of long, sick-looking red kelp like streaks of blood. This island is normally submerged, the Kelanua conclude, but the extraordinarily low tide means the sea level has fallen enough to expose the misshapen lump of land.

Captain Nakhona organizes repairs for the *Iron Eel*, but Alak'ai places all of the player characters on watch duty. Who knows what dangers may lurk here, out of sight of the mainland, on an island that usually lies beneath the surface? They all need to get off this rock as soon as possible.

[There's no combat here, and no crises, but this is a discrete section, a sequel – a rest stop – before the next scene, so it gets its very own section in my notes.]

[If you flip back to the second-level outline of this game, you'll see that I covered everything up to this point in only a handful of paragraphs. Even simple, single-sentence ideas can become full scenes. For all I know, it will take the entire first game session just to play through this much of my campaign notes.]

The Call of Cthulhu

While the player characters are keeping watch and the rest of the crew are repairing the *Iron Eel*, something reaches out to them. A mental force wells up, seeping across the island and prying at the thoughts of the frail-minded humans there.

The call is insidious and if the characters aren't on the lookout for such dangers, they may be taken unawares. Everyone needs to roll a mental stat + awareness-type skill with a small penalty. *[The penalty is because the mental attack is invisible and difficult to detect. Time for brainy characters to shine!]*

Each character that succeeds gains a small bonus to the next stage of the crisis. No bonus to those who fail, and a penalty only if someone critically fails the roll. *[The next part will be tough, so here we give characters a bonus for succeeding instead of a penalty for simply failing. If I start giving out too many penalties, then* no one *will succeed and that's discouraging for my players.]*

The call is like a song, though there's no actual sound. It's more like gravity – a subtle pull that lures all of the characters toward the center of the island. Roll a straight-up mental stat check to resist. *[Or whatever your RPG system uses to make rolls difficult. In a system with skills, not allowing use of those skills makes succeeding in the roll a real challenge.]*

Each character takes X sanity damage *[quite a bit here]* reduced by any success on their resistance roll. *[The PCs are under attack by madness, so madness is the cost of failure, but we give them some kind of mental roll to resist and lessen the damage.]*

All of the characters stumble a few steps forward, but any who resisted are able to snap themselves out of it. Player characters that fail and much of the NPC crew, though, continue to shamble on in a trance. Alak'ai and Hoka have also resisted the summons, and now they're calling to the crew to come back. The old sailor shouts to tie them up and Alak'ai obeys.

The characters can help stop crew – and any PCs that couldn't resist the magical call – with a physical stat + brawl or athletics skill (or maybe boating for knot-tying). If any of the player characters have been caught by the mystic force, they must roll a mental stat + survival or nature kind of skill to avoid shambling over sharp rocks, stepping onto a poisonous anemone, or tripping. They can't stop themselves from following the call, but they can try not to follow it right into a rock.

Those summoned by the call will resist being restrained. Each character that fails the roll to capture their friends takes X amount of damage in the struggle. *[A pretty small hit of damage here, since they may be already battered by the storm and they'll get more beat up by crab-men soon.]* Characters summoned by the call take X amount of damage *[also a low-value hit, for the same reasons]* if they fail and the inhospitable terrain scrapes and tears at them.

Within minutes, everyone who resisted the summoning has tied up everyone who didn't. But when Alak'ai takes a quick roll call, he determines that Danya is missing. She survived the storm and the shipwreck, but she's not among the crew now.

Captain Nakhona just waves a hand dismissively. Danya is only a prisoner and not worth searching for. And the girl has blue eyes… They're all better off without any sea-eyes watching them. Nakhona knows the ocean and knows better than to mess with anything on it or under it. And that includes this strange island. If Danya wants to wander off until she falls and breaks her neck or the tide covers this place and she drowns, then that's her fate.

But Hoka reminds his captain that they *all* felt the call. Whatever summoned them didn't do it for any good reason – and if they don't find Danya now, they may all regret it. Alak seconds the old sailor's opinion and Nakhona relents. He puts everyone else back to work, leaves a few Kelanua in charge of watching the prisoners, and leads the player characters – along with Alak'ai, Hoka and a few sailors – toward the island interior.

Search & Rescue

Everybody felt that eerie mental call, so they know which direction to go in search of Danya. Shouting her name, the party clambers over rocks and wades through tide pools following after her.

With a mental stat + alertness roll, they can catch sight of the Strazni girl shambling over the island ahead of them. If they hurry, maybe they can catch up to Danya before she goes too far. However, a successful roll also means catching sight of something else in the distance – a temple made of a dark green-black stone. The building is either crude or subtly elegant... Hard to say which, but the design certainly wasn't meant to please human sensibilities.

Any character who succeeded in the alertness roll must resist X amount of sanity damage.

[Quick aside on sanity damage. What happens when the characters lose all their sanity? How do they get it back? At zero sanity, the player gets to choose a derangement for their character – a mental problem like a phobia, a compulsion, or a nervous tic that they must now role-play and which may penalize them in certain situations. Sanity returns with rest and I might award bonus sanity for certain role-playing scenes if it makes sense – confiding in and bonding with a friend, for example. In other games, I've also offered crutches... and by that, I mean drugs. Characters received bonuses for drinking alcohol or taking narcotics, numbing their mind to the horrors they were forced to confront. But critical failure while relying on crutches or overusing them leads to in-character addiction.]

As the characters hurry to catch up to Danya, misshapen boulders festooned with barnacles and shredded kelp suddenly shift and move. They're not rocks at all – they're shells. Creatures that look like barely anthropomorphized crabs rise and scuttle toward the characters. The inhuman monsters let Danya pass unharmed, but viciously attack the PCs.

Combat map: Rocky area with tide pools. *[I want lots of difficult terrain here that will slow movement.]*

Sanity damage: These crab-monsters aren't supposed to exist and each character must resist X sanity damage.

NPC bonuses: Alak'ai fights with the PCs and provides a bonus attack to one player character each round.

Special rules: None in this fight.

Crab-men stats: There are two crab-men for each of the player characters. *[I can have more scuttle over the rocks or come out of a deep pool if the combat goes too quickly and I'm not ready for it to be over quite yet.]*

These things are going to make repeated appearances, so I don't want them to be too tough. They need to be a moderate challenge for starting characters, and easy kills for advanced characters when I bring them back at the end.

And in general, I would rather have my PCs cut through large numbers of smaller foes than one large one. I save the big enemies for special occasions. But these are crab-men, so they'll have good armor. I'll also give them soft underbellies, though, or gaps in their shells that the PCs can target to bypass the armor.

The crab-monsters' attacks will be pincher-based, though I also made one where they get that pincher around a limb or throat and squeeze. And with all of those extra legs, I'll make the crabs fairly mobile and give my players the opportunity to chase them over the slippery rocks.

Combat is over when all of the enemies are killed.

Temple of Doom

The crab-creatures slowed the characters down and by the time they hack their way through, they're even further behind Danya. They chase her toward the temple and Hoka probably doesn't have to point out that letting her get there would be a bad idea.

But the attack left them no choice – Danya has already reached the temple. Everyone can run, but as they watch, Danya touches the great doors and they swing open. She walks right through, into the darkness beyond.

Captain Nakhona wants to turn around and leave immediately. The damage is surely done, isn't it? But Alak'ai is willing to go in after the lost prisoner and Hoka argues that they can't let Danya be used for whatever she was brought here to do. Nakhona grumbles, orders torches and lanterns lit, then tells Alak'ai to take the lead as everyone goes inside.

The island temple is vast and the gray-green shadows swallow the weak torchlight as if hungry. Characters can barely make out twisted pillars and deep wall niches, and a stairwell on the far side leading steeply down. Every surface seems to be covered in carvings of closed eyes and mouths, and the walls look like they're made of partially melted wax.

Danya stands alone in the middle of the strange chamber, arms wrapped around herself and whimpering quietly. Alak motions for the other sailors to flank Danya so they can get around her and prevent her from reaching the stairs.

The characters may call out to Danya or approach her, and the girl will respond. She turns toward them, face streaked in tears, and eyes open but sightless. Her perceptions are not her own, but the player characters just might be able to get through to her if they are gentle and persistent.

One of the Kelanua sailors slowly approaching Danya suddenly screams. A closed mouth carved into the floor has opened and bit down on his leg. Everywhere across the temple, eyes and mouths are snapping open. The melted wax surface isn't the wall and floor, but some thick coating that oozes into swift and terrible motion. A pseudopod drips down from the ceiling and grabs another sailor, yanking them off into the shadowy upper reaches of the chamber.

Everyone must resist X amount of sanity damage. *[This one will be a big hit. It's the characters' first encounter with the shoggoth and it should leave a mark.]*

Captain Nakhona slashes out at the creature, but his cutlass just splashes harmlessly through it again and again. Then the blade gets stuck and dark slime surges up over Nakhona, smothering him as he screams in horror.

Hoka shouts for everyone to run and makes for the door as fast as he can, but a tooth-tipped tendril impales the old sailor and lifts him into the air. It shakes Hoka, spraying his blood through the air until his body flies off the tentacle in two separate pieces. Choking, Alak'ai takes up the call to flee.

Danya still stands in the chamber, moaning fearfully. The characters can snatch her and drag her out with a physical stat + brawl roll. Or a difficult social stat + social skill roll might snap Danya out of it and let her help herself.

[If the players don't seem inclined to save Danya, Alak'ai will give the order to do so. If they still want to leave her, he'll grab the girl before running... Though the PCs will lose some respect from Alak'ai for their inaction. I'm not too worried, though. My players do "heroic" very well.]

The PCs will need X amount of success to rescue Danya from the temple. *[I'll make this number fairly high so that all of my players need to contribute, or one player will have to really excel to manage it alone.]* For each success that they fall short, they take X amount of damage as gaping, fang-filled maws snap at them or pseudopods studded in claws strike out.

[I once again have a fail condition here where the PCs still succeed in the task, but at a cost. We need Danya for the rest of the game.]

The liquid horror bubbles and shudders, shaking the entire temple. A pseudopod lashes out, pulping another sailor and shattering a pillar. Chunks of stone go flying. Each character must make a physical stat + defense skill or be hit by debris or stumble into the gnashing mouths flowing around them. Danya is still stunned and can't defend herself, so someone must pull her out of harm's way, or put themselves between her and danger – and make the roll with a moderate penalty as a result.

A failed check means taking X amount of damage. If the character protecting Danya failed, they take slightly more damage.

The shoggoth is dripping down off the ceiling and temple walls, flowing over everything and the ooze is creeping rapidly toward the open doors. The characters must run, duck, dodge, jump, and hack their way through the riot of whipping tentacles. Physical stat + just about any physical skills can be used to escape. Whoever might be dragging or carrying Danya, though, has a small penalty.

A failed check deals X damage. Success is escape with no new wounds.

As the characters reach the doors, a tendril whips out and coils around Alak's leg. The first mate falls, fingers scrabbling for a grip as he's dragged back into the temple. He manages to catch the edge of the doors, but he won't be able to resist the thing's strength for long. The characters can hack at the tentacle or grab Alak and try to pull him through the doors. It takes a physical stat + athletics roll to pull Alak'ai out or a combat skill roll to cleave through the semi-liquid tendril holding him.

The players must accumulate X number of successes. For each success they fall short, they need to spend X resources [willpower, energy, healing surges, or whatever is used in your preferred RPG system] to strain and free Alak'ai.

[The characters have been through the storm crisis, mental crisis, the combat with the crab-men, and now the escape crisis. Even though there was only one traditional fight, see how beat up your characters are? Do they feel the tension? Was the chapter still exciting? This is why I like to mix in crisis scenes.]

Everyone bolts back across the island, fleeing the temple. Even if the characters shut the doors behind them, they burst open. The oozing monstrosity – Danya mumbles something about "Tekeli-li" over and over again – pours out of the temple like syrup. It slows as it flows into the bright daylight, uncountable eyes squeezing shut or sinking into the slick gray-black slime of its mass.

But within moments, they blink open again and resurface. The living liquid begins to flow out again. It covers the temple steps and the rocks, and keeps coming. Just how big is this creature?

The group can scramble over the rocks, back toward the edge of the island and Danya stumbles along with them now. Other than muttering *Tekeli-li* endlessly, she seems to have recovered a little and no longer needs to be carried.

["Tekeli-li" is a phrase that the shoggoth gibbered in a Mythos story, and was heard first in The Narrative of Arthur Gordon Pym of Nantucket *by Edgar Allen Poe. So rather than call my monster a* shoggoth, *I've decided to use that. From here on, I'll use both the terms* shoggoth *and* Tekeli, *but they refer to the same big evil monster.]*

When they reach the *Iron Eel*, Alak'ai shouts to get the ship back into the water, whether the repairs are finished or not. The crew and prisoners working on the boat obey the first mate immediately, though there are a few loud questions about where the captain and the others have gone.

The Tekeli spreads across the strange island behind them and the *Iron Eel* casts off only moments ahead of the surging monster. Alak'ai shouts out commands desperately and they set sail for The Hunter.

[In the second outline, I was going to have a repair/sailing crisis here, but I decided that the players have done enough crises and combats for now, so they get to escape the island without any further rolls. I can always improvise a crisis if I feel like this chapter was a little too short or easy.]

Chapter reward

This part is highly dependent on what system you're running. In a level-based system – like *Dungeons & Dragons (D&D)* or *Palladium* – I level characters up at the end of each chapter. They don't receive experience for fighting monsters or using skills. Neither do they get experience for role-playing scenes. Those things are part of the game and they'll just happen. I want my players focused on developing their personal character arcs and exploring the narrative that I created instead of trying to earn experience points. I level them up along with the story so they can enjoy new abilities and face greater threats.

In games where you earn and spend experience to raise stats or buy perks of one kind or another – like *White Wolf* or *Big Eyes, Small Mouth (BESM)* – all my players receive the same number of points. Some players are naturally shyer than others, and so I don't reward whoever spent the most time talking. Some players enjoy combat more than others, and I don't reward whoever got in the most fights. I don't reward or punish my players for taste.

Everybody gets the same experience and can spend it how they like. In level-based games, all of your stats tend to go up at once when you level, but when you spend experience, only the things you purchase advance. So I also hand out standard rewards each chapter, usually to combat-related skills or hit points/health pools. I want to make sure that all of the characters are ready for the greater threats in the next chapter.

Even if one of the players spends all of their experience into singing and drawing, I make sure to award the skills and increased survivability that the story will require from them. That way, my players don't have to worry about not being able to keep up and can focus instead on developing their character.

CHAPTER 2

The Hunter

The *Iron Eel* sails hard for the mainland. Repairs are half complete and the damaged ship leaks every league of the way. The crew has to make several more fixes as they travel, and the *Iron Eel* is shorthanded. Alak'ai is acting captain now and he has no choice but to put everyone to work – including any Antoran mercenaries.

It takes three days to sail back to The Hunter instead of the two that it took on the out-going mission. And the entire time, the creature from the temple chases them. It covers the island and seeps into the sea. The monster floats on the surface like an oil slick, eyes and mouths bubbling up and sinking into the gooey mass. It swims slowly against the current, but the creature is vast and powerful, engulfing waves with its bulk. It stretches for miles, swallowing the horizon.

Everyone works hard and is exhausted, but if the PCs need time to talk amongst themselves, they can converse between tasks.

Danya is shaken, but mostly recovered. Alak'ai will take pity on the girl and she's the only one not put to work. But Danya insists on doing what she can. She can't speak much about what happened to her in the temple, but she can at least confirm through knowledge she doesn't understand that the liquid beast slowly pursuing them is called a Tekeli. (A Tekeli, not *the* Tekeli, meaning there are more of those things out there somewhere...)

[This is our sequel, where the group can rest and recover and discuss what's happened, or make plans about what to do next. While Alak'ai is

pushing the crew and ship hard and there'll be more sequel time at the lighthouse, there's three days of sailing and no reason the PCs can't chat if they want. Or I can easily narrate the difficult journey and segue to land-fall, if they don't need the time.]

When the light of The Hunter sweeps out from the eastern horizon, a cheer goes up from the crew. By the time the *Iron Eel* reaches the lighthouse, the sentries have also spotted the black mass of the Tekeli spreading toward shore. Kelanua lighthouse guards are there to meet the ship and help the wounded sailors dock.

Alak'ai gives out some final orders, but then he demands to see The Hunter's Keeper of the Tower. He'll take Danya and the player characters with him. They're the only ones to enter the temple and get out alive. *[And I want them there to role-play the meeting. They're the stars of this show, not Alak.]*

Towerkeeper Lukoa has an office near the top of the lighthouse, just beneath the lamp room. Lukoa's office contains a pair of globes – one showing Tydalus at high tide and one at low tide – well-kept navigational equipment, a telescope, and shelves full of rolled-up maps. A row of windows look out west and the Tekeli spreads like a stain below, visible as a black line on the horizon.

Unless one of the players jumps in, Alak'ai can give an overview of what happened. It began as a standard fishing trip, including the encounter with the tentacle beast. The creature was more deformed than the sharks and squid that the Kelanua usually encounter at low tide, but not entirely unknown. But then the storm wrecked the ship. Alak'ai will be honest about Nakhona's mistakes while trying not to speak ill of the captain. He finishes with the shipwreck, then hands the report over to the rest of the characters, who can add any details they consider important.

Danya will tell Keeper Lukoa that she felt the song – something incomprehensibly large grabbing her mind and then pulling her to the temple. But after that, she doesn't recall anything until the PCs pulled her out of the temple.

Lukoa can question the other characters about what happened in the temple and how they escaped. After, Lukoa will light a pipe and think on what they said, but if the PCs have any other advice or suggestions, he'll listen.

When everyone has spoken their piece, Lukoa takes a mounted tube from the wall and then blows into it, sounding a whistle heard echoing through the lighthouse.

"This is Keeper Lukoa," he says. "Shine the warning light."

Alak'ai can explain what the hell that means for any inlander characters. Up in the lamp room, stunned Kels pause for a moment, and then leap into action. They crank open an aperture in the lamp room ceiling and slide a mirror into position to reflect light upward. A beam of light thrusts into the sky like a great glowing blade. Alak admits that he's never heard of a warning light at low tide. *[I decided on the up-pointing light instead of changing the color since the vertical beam would be more visible at a distance.]*

Keeper Lukoa tells Alak'ai that he is now captain of the *Iron Eel* and to get repairs underway immediately. Any mercenary characters will be paid their wage in salt, plus a small bonus for helping to get the ship back safely and bring this warning. The Hunter will soon be under attack, though, and the mercenaries are offered payment to stay and fight.

[I don't think that anyone in my gaming group would walk away at this point, but I can imagine a player declining Lukoa's offer and leaving. That's their prerogative, but it's obvious that this is the story of my game. If a character goes, then they're walking away from the story and you're under no obligation to make up something else. We offered the players a story, and that's the one we're telling. If they don't want to participate, then that's their decision. You can run short scenes of them leaving The Hunter, going up the road to the next town, but the only mercenary work this year is on the coast. Not much is going on – it's low tide, when everything is more or less safe – and the character needs to have a change of heart and turn around if they want any adventure.]

The Siege

Messengers are dispatched from The Hunter to the rest of the lighthouses and by now, other Kelanua must have seen The Hunter's warning light pierce the sky. But the Tekeli continues its inexorable crawl across the sea and will reach The Hunter before reinforcements do. It will take the Tekeli only another day to float across the sea and come within range of the coast.

During the wait, the Kelanua have preparations to make. They weren't expecting an attack from the sea. Their stores of weapons and supplies are as low as the tide. What they have will be rushed into position by the lighthouse crew and prisoners pulled off mine details. The player characters can rest and recover. If they have any preparations of their own to make, now is the time.

But the next day, the Tekeli seems to have suddenly and mysteriously stopped its advance toward shore. Every eyeglass and telescope in The Hunter is trained on its inky mass, so it's almost too late when the alarm bells sound an attack. The Tekeli still hasn't moved, but crab-monsters march up from the sea, climbing over the salt-encrusted rocks to scuttle toward and then up the tower. Kelanua rush through the lighthouse to engage the creatures as they climb, testing tightly shuttered windows and balcony ledges.

Combat map: Balcony backed by the lighthouse tower.

Sanity damage: Each PC must resist X sanity damage. *[Same as they took on the island before because it's the same monster.]*

NPC bonuses: Alak'ai provides a bonus attack to one character each round.

Special rules: I'll give the crabs an attack that lets them push the characters around and then shove them off the balcony. A physical stat + athletics roll will allow them to grab onto the edge and prevent a fall. Since I can't have player characters plummeting to their doom just yet – we're not that far through the story – the cost of failure here will be loss of a resource *[energy, healing surges, etc.]*

as they struggle back up to safety. Plus, the rest of the party has to fight without them until they succeed in getting up again.

Crab-men stats: There are two crabs for each character. *[I can have more scuttle up onto the balcony if the combat goes too quickly, but this is the second go against these things and I should have an idea how many will make a good fight.]*

The player characters are a level higher now or have spent some experience and chapter rewards since the last fight, so they're a bit more powerful. The differences won't be too noticeable yet, but the crab-men will be a little easier to defeat now. That's okay – we have several combats and crises to wear the characters down and make the siege feel harrowing.

Moments after the PCs fight off the wave of crab-men, Kelanua warriors arrive to back them up. They relieve the characters and hold the balcony. But Alak'ai points off to one side. The monsters have circled around to the east flank of the lighthouse where there are fewer defenses. He implores the player characters for further help to repel the attack – they are the only ones who have fought these things before.

Alak'ai rushes the group through the huge lighthouse and up long flights of stairs. The crab-men haven't climbed up this far – yet – but there aren't as many balconies on this inland flank of The Hunter. When the characters look down over the ledge, they can see the crab-monsters climbing over the huge old stones with their pointed legs.

Alak'ai knots a rope around his waist while a younger Kelanua is tying the other end to the railing. Coils of rope await the other characters. Alak tells them to lean forward and keep their feet on the tower – just pretend they're upright. He climbs over the railing and begins walking down the side of the lighthouse to do battle.

[This is more crab-monsters, so another combat here would just be the same enemies on a different map and that's going to get really old really fast. So this encounter will be a crisis.]

If any of the player characters have a phobia of heights, they take X sanity damage per level of their phobia. *[If the PCs began the game with or earned any derangements through sanity loss in Chapter 1, most of them tend to cause more sanity damage.]*

At low tide, the sides of the lighthouse are thankfully dry, but the tower is rounded and rappelling face-first down the outside is no easy challenge. Physical stat + athletics check to rappel down the lighthouse and reach the crab-men.

A failed roll means that the character loses their footing, slips, and bounces off the lighthouse or drops a few feet before suddenly jerking to a halt at the end of their tether. They take X amount of damage *[just a little this early in the crisis]*, and suffer a penalty on the next roll.

The characters walk down The Hunter's side to reach the crab-monsters and then must knock them off the sides. They can strike with weapons, or just try to kick them off the lighthouse. Physical stat + combat or athletics skill with any penalties from a failed roll on the previous stage.

A failed check means taking X damage from the crab-men as they fight back.

And then it's time for a mental stat + alertness skill!

A failed check imparts a penalty to act as they see one crab has managed to scuttle up the lighthouse and get above them. It comes around the side of the tower, meaning to cut their ropes. The PCs can stop it with a physical stat + combat skill or athletics. *[Since it will probably involve a ranged attack or climbing quickly up their own rope to engage it.]*

The character who rolled the worst on the alertness check has their rope cut! The other characters can grab them or their severed rope with a physical stat + athletics or brawl check.

Success on the roll results in a heroic and relatively effortless save. Failure means that they grab the rope, but friction burns tear their skin or the sudden stop half yanks their arm out of the socket.

The assisting PC and the falling character both take X damage and lose X other resource *[energy, willpower, healing surges, or something else along those lines]*.

[I could have the failure mean the character falls to their death. But honestly, I'd rather just beat the characters up and keep them around for the story. I gain nothing by killing a PC and then the player has to make a new character, then we have to work them into the story. That's a lot of work for zero profit.]

The crab-monsters have rallied and formed up. The creatures are ready to fight back, but clumping up close gives the player characters a chance to hit them hard and knock the whole bunch off the lighthouse. Alak'ai shouts for a charge and slides down his rope to smash into them. The PCs roll a physical stat + athletics or combat skill with a penalty to safeguard this front.

Failure means that the crab-men get to inflict X damage as they fight back.

The character who rolled the worst in the check above knocks the final crab off the lighthouse, but it grabs onto their ankle. Its weight threatens to pull their foot right off or snap their rope. The other player characters may try to hack the crab claw off one at a time (they can roll initiative if they all want to go first) with a physical stat + combat skill check.

If the first character to help fails their skill check, the grabbed character takes X damage, and then the next helper can try. Each failure means the grabbed character takes X damage until they are cut free, or they take enough damage to be incapacitated and take a scar.

[Rather than have a PC die at zero health and lose a character in the story, it's more fun to give them a defect and let them keep playing – in this case a missing foot seems appropriate, or maybe a phobia of crustaceans or heights. Not all scars are physical, after all.]

Signs & Portents

Kelanua on the east balcony haul the characters back up and then help them into the tower. They get only a short break, listening to sounds of distant fighting up and down the lighthouse.

Danya wanders into the room as if sleepwalking. She mumbles that the cries of the Tekeli have woken the Dekara *[I'm getting tired of calling these things "crab-men" and I want to give them a better name, so I derived this term from* decapod, *the order that crabs belong to]*, who once built cities of shell above and below the waves until the apes learned to use tools and stole the land from them.

Danya shuffles past, toward the balcony outside and will walk straight off unless restrained, though it doesn't take a dice roll to do so. She shakes herself awake and is sincerely glad to see her friends have survived the attack. Danya doesn't remember what she said, but she knows the crab-things hate humans and everything warm-blooded.

Alak'ai asks how Danya knows these things, but she insists that she doesn't. Talking about it quickly gives her a headache, though the Strazni girl is willing to at least try to think of anything that might help The Hunter and all the people living inside. And there *is* something... Danya says that the Tekeli fears "the Sign..."

But she doesn't know what that means. Before the players can ponder the problem too long, new alarm bells ring. Alak'ai pushes himself to his feet wearily, but grabs his weapons. That alarm is for a breach. Something has broken into the lighthouse.

The characters follow Alak and the bells. Soon they're joining a flow of armed Kelanua. The Dekara – if that's what the crab-men are called – have broken through a mining tunnel and poured into an interior room.

Combat map: Interior chamber with narrow hallway or stairs. *[Part of this map will have some maneuvering room, but the other half will be tight and present some mobility challenges for my players.]*

Sanity damage: Learning the name of the Dekara doesn't help human minds accept them any easier. Each PC must resist X sanity damage.

NPC bonuses: Alak'ai provides a bonus attack to one character each round.

Danya has also followed her friends into this battle. She doesn't fight, but she does shout warnings to the characters. She seems to know just when the Dekara are going to attack and when to duck their massive serrated pincers. She allows one character to re-roll a single attack or defense each round.

[Danya now has a token on the board. While I'll have Alak'ai – who is a warrior – help the characters to flank enemies or block approaches, Danya won't. But I can surround or threaten her, forcing my players to take action to protect her. I won't make any rolls for Danya – like Alak, she doesn't even have a character sheet.]

Dekara stats: There are four Dekara on the map for each player character. *[I want to ramp up the danger now.]*

I can up the ante again by introducing larger Dekara – which I think I'll call *hard-shells* – a heavier breed with greater strength and armor. And more ability to push, so I can bash the PCs into those close stone walls.

Tekeli-li

If my players are up for rushing into another combat, then there is no pause. Even while Kelanua reinforcements push the invading Dekara back through the breach and pour boiling pitch through the crack to clear it, the characters hear a new bell tolling.

If the player characters are too beat up for another fight, then the Kelanua clear the breach and get to work sealing it back up. The Dekara attack falters and the few remaining creatures fight to the last, but are cut down one by one. I won't have the Tekeli attack until the next day.

Either way, the warning light shines up into the cloudy sky like a pillar of light, though there are no ships yet. But the black slick of the Tekeli begins to move once again. Alak'ai has a spyglass and will pass it around the group so they can get a look.

The main mass of the huge Tekeli remains a few miles out, but the inky edges ripple and begin to stretch and deform. Tendrils a dozen yards thick reach out, then break off from the Tekeli like dividing amoeba. A hundred individual black blobs – each of them tiny compared to the vast creature that spawned them, but still ten yards across at the smallest to the size of a ship at largest – swim on their own toward The Hunter.

All of the player characters take X sanity damage from the sight of the Tekeli spawning.

The Hunter's trebuchets and mangonels fire. *[A mangonel is also called a* traction trebuchet, *made for knocking down castle walls but probably also a good weapon for giant sea monsters. I had never heard of mangonels until I read Robert E. Howard, who was writing buddies with Lovecraft. His stuff has got a lot of Mythos feel to it as well, so borrowing from him is almost as good as borrowing from Lovecraft.]*

Hurled stones fly out and splash into the shallow, low-tide sea, but several strike their targets. The black blobs splash, but instantly reform. The Hunter launches barrels of flaming pitch next, and the Tekeli amoebae seem to shrink in on themselves, shying away from the fire.

Cheers go up as something *finally* seems to be effective, but The Hunter's stores are sparse. During high tide, weapons are stockpiled to fight back the sea and the horrors that come with it, but between tides the inventory is low and even the Kelanua – many too young to have seen a Grandfather tide – have lowered their guard. The fire barrage stops many of the smaller Tekeli, but it won't last for long.

As if to remind The Hunter's defenders that they are not safe, a few of the amoebae ooze past the line of fire, changing shape to swim between pools of floating flame, and begin to move up the rocks toward the base of the lighthouse. As the Tekeli spawn reach The Hunter, its defenders pour hot oil and burning pitch down the sides. Again, flame seems effective, but the Kelanua have already used much of their stock against the Dekara.

[In the previous outline of this game, I planned on a siege weapon crisis, but just writing all of this out is already exhausting me. If it's tiring to write, it's going to be tiring to play. While I do want to capture the desperation of a siege and weariness of constant battle, actual constant fighting (well, role-played constant fighting) gets boring. We've already had multiple combats and crises without a sequel. So I can describe the large-scale weaponry at work – demonstrating the important information, that fire deters the Tekeli – then move on.]

The Hunter's warning bell rings and this time, the PCs recognize the breach alarm again. One of the Tekeli spawn has gotten into The Hunter!

Kelanua rush to the new breach in the lower levels of the lighthouse. The tower is built large and tall enough to stand above the high-water line at full tide when Grandfather Moon appears, so it's massive. Running down flights of stairs would take too long, but shafts running through the lighthouse let the Kels ride ropes down deeper into The Hunter.

All of the player characters will need to make a physical stat + athletics skill check to ride the ropes down a dozen stories or more. They have a moderate penalty to initiative, reduced for each success on their rope-riding roll.

Combat map: Interior store room.

Sanity damage: Each character must resist X sanity damage at the sight of the Tekeli spawn... and the sound of its multiple voices, endlessly whispering obscenities, the only intelligible of which is "Tekeli-li..."

NPC bonuses: Alak'ai provides a bonus attack to one character each round, and Danya lets one character re-roll a single attack or defense each round.

Special rules: Danya *will* give out her NPC bonus, but on the first round of combat, she just clutches her head and moans, unable to provide her bonus. On the second round, though, Danya pulls herself together enough to help.

If any of the player characters want to take supportive action – give Danya some kind of encouragement or help – then maybe a social stat + social skill roll will unlock her NPC bonus on the first round.

At the beginning of the third round, some Kelanua arrive with torches, lugging barrels of pitch. The gurgling Tekeli spawn quickly lashes out, decapitating one of them, scattering the reinforcements, and causing them to drop the supplies – but giving the characters access to pitch and fire.

The characters may coat their weapons in pitch and light them, fling burning tar at the spawn or something else. Hopefully, they'll be brave and creative. Depending upon what they do it might take their whole action, or I might let them do something quicker.

Tekeli spawn stats: Place a single token on the map, regardless of number of players. One will be plenty.

Multiple attacks or area-of-effect attacks that can hit more than one PC will be important. I want the Tekeli spawn to be dangerous and for the PCs to limp away afterward, maybe even get knocked down to zero health and take some defects.

As for taking damage, this thing is going to be liquid, so swords and arrows and any weapons the player characters might have are going to splash right through it, doing no more than half damage. Once they get some fire into play their attacks will do full damage, but I'm going to cheat here. I'll give the Tekeli spawn some amount of health, but even if the characters all score critical hits, I'm not going to call it dead until they get flame going.

Oh! Idea! Maybe if they beat the spawn to zero health without fire, it splits in two and both halves regenerate. Only fire will affect it without causing it to multiply.

Even when the PCs beat the spawn down to zero health with fire, it doesn't die. The amoeba only *retreats*. Yep, all their blood and sweat, and they only made it run away.

White Sails

Depending upon how long the rests between scenes needed to be, the player group has been fighting all day or for several days. The swarm of Tekeli spawn try to shift and swim around the flaming bombardment and slowly push the line back toward the shore of Korvath. The Tekeli itself moves behind its spawn, reaching out and reabsorbing them as it nears the lighthouse. It won't be long now until The Hunter is overwhelmed.

But then fire blooms on the Tekeli's northern flank. At the edge of the horizon, sails are just visible. The Kelanua have come from the other lighthouses – The Navigator and The Dolphin, The Fishhook and The Shark's Mouth. Their ships launch a new barrage of fire and the Tekeli – screaming and gibbering from thousands of mouths – shudders and rolls back out to sea like an angry wave.

The reinforcements push the Tekeli back, but it doesn't leave, and their barrage doesn't seem to be inflicting any serious damage. The monstrosity is held at bay, but not defeated. Alak'ai wonders how such a horror can possibly be defeated. Danya rocks herself, arms wrapped around her body, and mumbles again that the Tekeli fears only "the Sign."

Chapter reward

Same as in the first chapter. Level the player characters up or give out enough experience to buy some skills, along with a boost to health or maybe their sanity pool. Things are going to get tougher, and so the PCs need to as well.

CHAPTER 3

Wild Gull Chase

The Tekeli – an immense, amorphous evil black blob with eyes and fanged maws ceaselessly emerging and disappearing in its mass – was accidentally freed from a strange temple on a reef island laid bare by historically low tides. Miles across, this obscenity of nature – if it is natural at all – spreads across the surface of the ocean, and is held back from the land only by a faltering siege line of fire on the water. The lighthouse stores can't hold out forever, even with help from the other Kelanua. Something must be done before The Hunter is overwhelmed and the Tekeli spreads onto the land.

[This is a recap of the story so far. Again, I don't really read it out to my players word for word. But it's a quick way to start the game off and get everyone back up to speed.]

It may have been a relatively quiet night, but the characters feel like they've had only a few hours of rest when they're woken once more by Alak'ai. The *Iron Eel's* new captain has been summoned by Keeper Lukoa – and so have the inlander mercenaries and/or prisoners that escaped the temple.

In Lukoa's office high in the lighthouse, they find the Keeper of the Tower gazing at the sea through his telescope. The huge Tekeli is visible even to the unaided eye as a dark stain across the ocean, rising and swelling and washing out in ways that don't even try to mimic natural ocean waves. Danya turns her head away from the sight and remains on the eastern side of the room, as far from the Tekeli as she can get.

At a distance, the Tekeli causes no sanity damage, but if any of the PCs decide to check it out through the telescope or a spyglass, they take X sanity damage. *[Hey, they asked for it.]*

Keeper Lukoa reiterates that their weapons can't kill the Tekeli and holding it back is the best they can do. The Hunter is receiving support from the other lighthouses. They have requested supplies from the cities, too, but getting the Antorans to send aid is likely to be an argument. The inlanders don't take the sea seriously enough at high tide, let alone at an all-time low. Keeper Lukoa doesn't even bother to pardon any offense to the mercenaries.

So if Kelanua or Antoran weapons can't stop the Tekeli's spread, they must find something that will. Danya whispers about the Sign again, which Lukoa doesn't catch. The prisoner remains otherwise quiet, but if the player characters bring up what she said, Lukoa will grill Danya about it, though the young Strazni woman can't answer any of his questions.

Either way, the lighthouse commander is sending them to The Nautilus, the first and oldest of the Kelanua lighthouses. Their best lore-masters are there and what few Kelanua writings exist are kept in the Nautilus' library. If there's information about anything that can defeat the Tekeli – or what this "Sign" might be – then the lore-keepers of The Nautilus will be their best bet to find out.

Lukoa places Alak'ai in charge of the mission. Danya and any prisoners are to go with him, and he'll offer the mercenaries a job. They survived the Tekeli on the island and then the siege of The Hunter. Any prisoner characters don't get a choice and they don't get paid, but it's within Lukoa's power to commute their sentence. This mission will earn them their freedom.

As soon as repairs to the *Iron Eel* are completed, they'll all sail north to The Nautilus.

[I begin most of my chapters with a sequel – the rest between scenes – to let the players get warmed up and back into their characters. Starting right off with some action can pump them up or impart a jolt of energy.

Most of the time, though, my players don't want that. They need a bit of sequel time to get rolling before I juice things up. If they get back into character quickly, I have the option to drop in a combat or crisis earlier, story permitting.]

For any characters who are low on sanity, they can get a drink – vodka is the most common alcohol in Tydalus – or they can try out a traditional Kelanua cure. Because the Kels spend more time on the sea than anyone else, they have developed their own method.

The ocean is the problem, but it has also provided the solution. The dreamcap is a small, bioluminescent jellyfish that lives in the seas of Tydalus. Dreamcap have a psychotropic sting and Kelanua apothecaries keep them in barrels in the lighthouses, as well as on their ships. The sting is painful at first, but then it creates a dreamy sense of peace and euphoria that dulls the nightmares and trauma of life on the coast.

Any takers?

Setting Sail

The characters have one day to rest and gear up for a voyage and a mission to save the world. Alak'ai needs to check on repairs to the *Iron Eel* – he's nervous as its new captain – but he'll have time to speak to any of the characters that wish to, at meals if nothing else. Danya is afraid, but she trusts the player characters. They make her feel safe.

[There might not be a lot to discuss about the story right now. Most of what they have are mysteries at this point. But between Alak'ai and Danya, there are a pair of potential romantic interests to chat up and flirt with. If no one has any social scenes to play, though, then the day of preparation and much of the trip will be summed up with "you sail for X number of days" or something. But when the story presents some downtime, I always pause to give the players a chance to fill that interlude with personal or romantic story arcs.]

Early the next morning, the *Iron Eel* sets out for The Nautilus. The fire bombardment from other Kelanua ships intensifies to give the ship cover and the Tekeli retreats a little. Within two hours, the *Iron Eel* clears the miles-wide mass of the Tekeli and makes it out into the open sea. The sails unfurl and the wind, at least, is with the ship. The Nautilus is just over a week away.

[I did some half-assed Googling here for sailing times. I figure that Korvath is about the size of Europe, and it takes something like three weeks to sail the European coast. With thirteen lighthouses, we can say each one is about two days apart under ideal sailing conditions. Storms, sea monsters and things like that will factor in... But for the most part, I'll keep my players away from maps and distract them with shiny things. Or horrible things, in this case. I want them focused on the story, not the cartography.]

The *Iron Eel* passes The Fishhook – another Kelanua lighthouse – on the second day, and then The Navigator on the fourth. The Dolphin is the next lighthouse to the north, but on the fifth day, something glows in the water. It's an orb about the size of a human head that shines beautifully, full of color and warmth.

But then it rises out of the water on a gray-green stalk. Is it just another horror from the sea... or something called up by the Tekeli as the Dekara were? The characters have no way to know and can only fight for their lives as the rest of the monster slithers up from the deep, dark water.

Combat map: Sea, ship deck. *[This is the same map that I used in Chapter 1, actually. I love it when I get to reuse a map.]*

Sanity damage: Each character must resist X sanity damage. *[I'll deal a large lump here. The player characters have had the chance to rest up, but now it's time to start battering away their sanity pools again. If I'm lucky and have been able to build up the maddening atmosphere of Tydalus, sanity loss is probably as bad as regular damage. My characters might even rather take normal damage than be driven slowly out of their minds.]*

NPC bonuses: Alak'ai provides a bonus attack to one character each round, and Danya lets one character re-roll a single attack or defense each round.

Special rules: On round two, the waves surging outward from the sea monster's thrashing body rock the *Iron Eel* and knock over a barrel. Tiny, glowing dreamcap jellyfish go sloshing across the deck. One dreamcap sting helps blunt trauma, but now is not a good time to be high on jellyfish.

All of the player characters will need to make a physical stat + athletics roll to avoid getting stung. Anyone who fails the check will take X damage *[a small amount, since the dreamcaps don't exactly have knives on the end of their tiny little tentacles]* and an ongoing penalty to all attacks and defenses as the drug-like sting takes effect. They can roll a pure mental stat *[or saving throw or whatever]* at the end of each turn to shake off the dreamcap stupor.

Sea serpent stats: I don't want to just use the Dekara again here. It's time for something new, and I found some great art of a sort of angler fish-inspired dragon. Sounds just like the kind of thing that haunts the oceans of Tydalus, so I've created a sea serpent with a glowing lure. That lure will deal sanity damage and draw the characters in, then I can hit them with a big bitey attack.

I'll use just one of these angler dragons, but to keep the PCs on the move, it will submerge at the end of each round and pop up at a new place around the ship. The characters will have to run across the pitching deck to resume their attack.

Once they beat the sea serpent down to zero health, it sinks into the ocean. It's not clear if the beast is actually dead... but it doesn't emerge again.

The Nautilus

The *Iron Eel* sails north, leaving blood in its wake. But the ship and its crew fared well against the serpent monster, largely due to the fighting skill of the characters. They pass The Dolphin safely and two days later, finally arrive at The Nautilus.

[Remember to pause long enough for anyone who wants to role-play. If no one does, just move on to the next scene.]

The Nautilus is shorter and wider than The Hunter, and a little cruder. It was the first lighthouse built after the Kelanua drove the Cthyan barbarians into the sea, raised to guard against their return – and against other watery nightmares from the depths. At night, the lighthouse points up to the Nautilus constellation, a spiral of glittering silver stars in the sky that give the first Kelanua guard post its name.

[If the players are at all curious, Alak'ai can give some history on the lighthouses and how they were constructed. But Alak'ai can also do some stargazing to point out the Kelanua constellations – which probably have different names than the Antorans (mostly the Massir) gave them. Star-watching is some high-grade flirting material – leaning over shoulders to point up into the sky – and will make for some good romance-building on the trip.]

[In fact... I think I'll lean on that to do some character development for Alak'ai. Aside from being a sailor and warrior, he loves the stars. Yes, Grandfather Moon is terrible and there are tales of horror from the stars – like the dread planet Yuggoth and such – but there have to be good places, as well. After all, there are inhospitable islands in the ocean, but many of them are beautiful. Now Alak can reference the stars a lot and has some-thing to talk about besides the plot. It will make him a more well-rounded character and I can leverage it for romance if anyone is giving the young captain eyes.]

The *Iron Eel* has sent coded messages ahead with lanterns – just as the lighthouses can communicate by flashing patterns with their lights – and The Nautilus is expecting Captain Alak'ai and his crew. Alak and the player characters are taken into the old tower to speak with Keeper Mairanda. She's a gray-haired Kelanua woman built just like her lighthouse – short, thick and tough.

Flashing lights isn't a fast method of communication and limits the content of messages, so Mairanda asks for details. I'll give any player character the chance to step in and tell the story, but if no one is feeling that talkative, then Alak'ai briefs Mairanda. Once she has been brought up to speed on the problem, Mairanda sends for Mel'ai, the oldest lore-master of The Nautilus.

Mel'ai is Mairanda's uncle and a truly ancient man. He was the Keeper of the Tower before Mairanda and personally knows over a thousand Kelanua songs. The oral history and lore of their people is passed down in song, from their creation myths in Sulaweya to songs that teach children how to tie proper knots.

Mel'ai will listen to the descriptions of the Tekeli and Dekara, and then nod. He knows a song about an ancient power that even the Cthyans feared.

> A gift from beyond
> An ancient scribe
> During darkness long
> Shall turn the tide

[Creating songs, poems and riddles isn't my strong suit. But it doesn't have to be great music to be immersive. Just having the song goes a long way toward drawing my players into the narrative. I can't sing worth a damn, so I'll settle for sort of chanting this. Thankfully, I'm not giving myself a long song to perform.]

Unfortunately, that's as much of the song as Mel'ai knows. His grandfather taught him that verse, but most of the song was already forgotten. When the Antorans invaded Korvath, their ensuing war killed nearly eighty percent of the Kelanua people. Oral traditions take time to pass on and much of their songs and lore was lost.

At the end of the war – when the tide came in and both sides were trying to fight off the monsters from the ocean – there was an Antoran who took an interest in preserving the fading Kelanua lore.

He was a Massir man named Alhazred and when he realized that the Kels were going to be wiped out, he wanted to save some part of their culture. He learned the Kelanua tongue and transcribed thousands of songs.

Alhazred's collection of Kelanua songs was written down in his native Massir, but in the ages since the war, some of them have been translated into Antoran. And as the Kelanua learned the invaders' languages, they translated the transcribed songs from Massir back into Kelanua. The Nautilus library contains the complete works of Alhazred and the group is welcome to read through them.

[Yet more world building occurs naturally as I try to figure out how to get the characters some vital information. And yeah, Alhazred is a tribute to Abdul Alhazred of Lovecraft's writing.]

The Nautilus has a small library. The Kelanua have learned to read and write, but they still do most of their teaching and preserve their history through oral tradition. The Nautilus' library has some books about sailing, navigation, astronomy, and what few books have been written about their culture – mostly by Antoran scholars.

The library includes Alhazred's complete set of Kelanua songs, though when the characters reach for one book – a slender volume with yellowed pages and bound in old, stained skin – Mel'ai shouts a warning in Kelanua and gestures them away. That book is the Azif, Alak'ai or Mairanda can translate, which was also written by Alhazred. But it was the last manuscript that the scholar produced and penning it destroyed his mind. The Azif contains nothing good. *[The Necronomicon was also known as the Al Azif in Lovecraft's work.]*

Though The Nautilus' library is small, it still contains hundreds of books and will take many hours – if not days – to read through them all. Even with the help of Mel'ai, Alak, and the other Kelanua lore-masters, it will require a mental stat + lore or research check to comb through the library.

Characters that don't speak Kelanua or Massir make the roll at a substantial penalty. The best they can do is memorize the Kelanua or Massir word for *sign* or *scribe*, and then go through the books line by line until they recognize it.

The player characters get one roll each in-game day, but when they have accumulated X successes, they find a few useful passages, enough to rebuild the song. It's not perfect... These songs were old and were then translated into Massir, then translated back into Kelanua a hundred years later, so there may be some distortion.

But the song tells the story of a place in Korvath loathed by the Cthyans. A power was said to lie there that was feared by the Deep Ones, the Flying Polyps, and the Elder Things. Kelanua warriors searched for the weapon/power/sign, but either returned empty-handed, or not at all.

In the song, the Kelanua searched for a place where the skies were bright with the aurora, but where the sight did not drive humans to insanity. The most likely choice seems to be Vanhome, the northernmost city-state of Korvath. It was the very first mountaintop conquered by the Antorans and remains an important city to this day. *[Guess who just had to name a new location?]*

Did the Kelanua fail to find the weapon? Has it been long-since buried in quakes or washed away by the tide? Did it ever really exist at all?

There's no way to know except to be the next to search for the Sign. It's a slim hope, but may be the only one left for the people of Korvath.

Inland

The characters are heading inland now. Alak'ai is still ostensibly in charge of the mission, but they are leaving the sea and the Kelanua lighthouses behind. The Kelanua once ruled all of Korvath, but that was a long time ago and Alak'ai knows nothing of the mainland or Antoran ways. He's going to rely heavily on the inlander members of the group for guidance.

[Here even more than before, Alak will step back while the PCs make the decisions and do the talking. Here, in inland Korvath, he's viewed as just a crazy Kel instead of a respected ship captain.]

The party sets out heading east, following the winding mountain roads. Vanhome is one of the thirteen Antoran city-states and weeks away on foot. Danya is from Athol, a lower peak village of Vanhome, but she has little good to say about her hometown and isn't excited about going back.

Alak is in good condition and can walk tirelessly, but he's used to sailing and the slow travel frustrates him. How do the inlanders tolerate it? Besides, fire will only keep the Tekeli at bay for so long and The Hunter needs help as soon as possible.

It's only a four-day walk to the nearest city, Ashmont. It's a fairly heterogeneous city, with extensive Strazni, Bhataari, and Massir neighborhoods... Though they don't include the Kelanua in that cosmopolitan lifestyle and will not treat Alak'ai well. But Ashmont has something the characters badly need: horses.

The Antorans brought horses with them when their own continent was sinking. There isn't nearly as much open land in Korvath, however, so they've never been able to keep the animals in large numbers. Horses are still useful for land travel, so they've been bred sturdy to adapt to the mountains – but they're expensive. Mounts will triple the group's traveling speed, but they'll cost X amount of money. *[I'll charge something that's either just out of the group's price range or will practically bankrupt them.]*

The characters can buy horses in Ashmont with a social stat + social skill roll to haggle the price. They'll have a penalty for Alak'ai and any other Kels in the group, though, unless they're sent away or the characters treat them like shit. Appropriate role-playing can remove the penalty.

Of course, the people of Ashmont – horse traders included – aren't going to speak well of Alak or any other Kelanua characters.

In case the players stick up for them too much, I'll jot down some stats for angry Antoran townsfolk.

Combat map: Narrow, stone city streets.

Sanity damage: None.

NPC bonuses: Alak'ai provides a bonus attack to one character each round. But Danya doesn't give an NPC bonus in this combat because she has no special insight on humans and no intuitive aid to offer.

Special rules: None.

Angry townspeople stats: Humans armed with clubs, maybe some knives. I'll use some combined fire rules – not rolling dozens of attacks, but rolling for enemies in groups of three to six with a bonus to hit and damage.

The Ashmont townsfolk won't be tough enemies and will run away if badly hurt.

When the fight is over, a mounted Bhataari constable rides onto the scene. If the characters have killed anyone, they will be ordered to lay down their weapons and surrender. If they didn't, the constable still wants to know what happened. In his opinion, only an idiot picks a fight with trained mercenaries, but he's just as biased as anyone else in Ashmont and won't side with the Kels.

The characters will be able to talk their way out of trouble, but if they killed anyone in the fight, it takes a bribe to make the constable look the other way. Regardless, the party is told to get out of Ashmont by the end of the day.

If all goes well in Ashmont and there is no fight, then the characters may buy a few horses (they can save money by doubling up on the mounts – an opportunity to pair up potential romantic partners) and be on their way at speed.

If they got themselves kicked out of Ashmont or chose not to buy horses, then they can move on toward Vanhome on foot.

Vanhome

Vanhome is built on a tall, narrow mountain, settled mostly by the Strazni. They are fiercely independent and untrusting of outsiders. Danya was born in Athol, one of Vanhome's villages, and her outgoing nature was part of the reason she never fit in there. Vanhome is insular enough that they wouldn't send supplies to their lighthouse on the coast if it wasn't absolutely necessary, but the other Antoran city-states pressure them to carry their share of supporting the Kelanua lighthouses.

Fortunately, the characters don't have to go into Vanhome itself – Danya warns them that it would be a challenge even convincing them to let outsiders in through the gates – but will need to search the lower peaks. The song that they researched in Alhazred's books says that the northern slopes of the mountain were shunned by the Cthyans.

All of those Kelanua searchers explored this mountain during their reign, and the Antorans have established their own towns and villages in the centuries since, changing the face of the mountain. It could take weeks to explore the entire thing, but they don't have to. The characters can ask around about any mysterious places or local legends about the mountain.

A village just above the high-water mark called Dunspire offers supplies and beds, and might be a good base from which the group can conduct their search. Danya's never been to Dunspire, but she's from this area and can suggest going there. Alak'ai will make the player characters take the lead and do the talking. After their experiences up in Ashmont, he doesn't want any trouble, and even if the people of Dunspire aren't as bigoted as in Ashmont, most inlanders don't have any love for the Kelanua.

Dunspire *[named after Lovecraft's Dunwich]* is a small village situated beside a river running down the mountainside. The town is almost quaint and built up around a well-maintained church.

[If you've read any Lovecraft or the work that he inspired, then you know that quaint little towns with churches are a big, blinking warning sign.]

There's no gate to prevent the group from entering Dunspire and they're not stopped, but the townspeople watch the newcomers silently and no one greets them. If the players speak to any of the locals, they are met with the bare minimum of courtesy, but also with some answers to their questions.

No one in Dunspire claims to know about any local legends or mysterious artifacts, though. If the characters try asking around at the Dunspire church, they're allowed inside the outer chamber, but sealed stone doors keep them out of the true interior. A Zelletaran priest welcomes them more warmly than anyone else so far and will listen to their mission, but regrets that he can't help.

A mental stat + alertness or investigation skill check will show that the remote Zelletaran church bears no images of either Zelleny or Rhystar. There are scenes of sunken cities and looming waves, but the buildings don't look like the old cities of Antora.

If questioned, the priest explains it all away by saying that the pictures show the artists' best idea of what old Massir and Strazni cities looked like (the Bhataari were nomads and didn't build very many cities), and can't be blamed for their imagination. Dunspire's idols of Zelleny and Rhystar are all in the inner sanctum, which is exclusive for members of the church. They're a small branch of the Zelletar religion, the priest says, and their ways may seem a little odd to worshipers of larger sects.

[I figure that any major religion has at least a handful of different sects. Some see Zelleny and Rhystar as mortals, others as avatars of the Mother and Father Moons, some who say they were born mortal but were elevated to divinity after their martyrdom. And so on.]

Dunspire has a single small inn. Vanhome may be insular, but they do get travelers and people sometimes stop in Dunspire on their way up the slope. Accommodations aren't spacious or lavish, but the innkeeper will hand out keys for the small, drafty rooms and the price is reasonable. *[I'll set my price at something affordable, even if the characters spent most of their money on horses. Worst-case scenario, I'll have the priest walk in and ask for a discount for the players in the name of their quest and of Zelleny and Rhystar. The innkeeper agrees without question.]*

Curse Your Sudden But Inevitable Betrayal

The characters are sent to the third floor of the tall and narrow inn. Their rooms are all adjacent and there don't seem to be any other guests on this floor. Or any other guests at all. The whole inn is quiet but for wind whispering through cracks in the walls.

Later that night, the Dunspire villagers gather together around the inn bearing torches, knives, and clubs. Outsiders aren't welcome here, and their questions have earned the strangers some... special treatment. The villagers creep up the inn to the third floor in the early hours of the morning.

The PCs should all be asleep and unarmed, but they can make a mental stat + alertness check with a penalty. If any characters have a plausible reason for being up past midnight, then they can make the roll without the penalty. Anyone who succeeds hears the murmur of voices from the villagers outside or the approach of the ones using the skeleton key to unlock the first door.

Each player character reduces the penalty on the next stage of the crisis for every success on their alertness check. Failure means they take the whole penalty.

So many feet and hushed voices will eventually wake even the deepest sleepers and the characters can react as the door to the first room begins to open. *[I can roll at random to determine whose room the villagers are coming into.]* The PC can make physical stat + athletics checks to bar the door with furniture. They have a penalty for going from sleep into action mitigated by their success to wake up above.

For the character whose room was first targeted, a failed check means that one of the villagers gets an arm or weapon through the door long enough to take a swing before the PC can bar their way. The character takes X damage.

For characters in the next rooms down, they have time to bar their doors before the villagers try to force them. But if they fail their roll, they're too slow and suffer a penalty on the next stage.

With furniture blocking the doorways, there's only one way to leave the inn rooms – the windows. Alak'ai will shout for everyone to climb up to the roof, but the characters need to gather their gear or else leave it behind. A mental stat + athletics or maybe melee roll lets them grab up their gear before the villagers of Dunspire break through. Characters that failed the stage above have a penalty.

Every character owns armor, weapons, and miscellaneous gear. Each level or point of success on the athletics check allows them to gather up one category of items. (Not necessarily to strap them on, just to scoop it up.) If they don't have enough success to collect all of their gear, the player chooses what gets left behind. *[You can break it down further if you want, potentially even asking for each item in the characters' inventory, but that seems like a bit much to me.]*

Sneaking into their rooms and just grabbing the outsiders one by one is no longer an option, so the villagers are pounding on all the doors now. Outside the window, the characters can see the mob looking and pointing up at them.

Alak'ai shouts to climb and starts up the side of the building. Each player character must make a physical stat + athletics check to scale the building and reach the roof. They have a small penalty for carrying their gear while trying to climb, and anyone with a phobia of heights takes some sanity damage.

Failing the roll deals X damage from hurled stones, knives, and torches the mob flings up at them as the characters make for the roof. *[I considered having the PCs drop some gear if they failed, potentially leaving them with nothing if the player's dice screwed them over.*

Maybe they could steal their stuff back, but this crisis is already a little more complex than usual, so I'm going to keep things simpler.]

Up on the roof, the characters can hear the doors and furniture splintering as the villagers break through. Other members of the mob begin climbing the inn walls, coming after the characters. Alak suggests getting out of Dunspire immediately, but they have to lose the mob first. The group can flee from roof to roof with a physical stat + athletics roll.

Not all of the roofs are at the same height as the inn's. A failed check means that the character makes a hard landing. They take X amount of damage and suffer a penalty to the next stage.

The PC party has now gained enough of a lead to vanish. They must make a physical stat + stealth skill check to slip from sight and then to remain quiet as the pursuing mob spreads out to search for the strangers.

A failed roll means that the character is almost discovered by one of the searchers. They may spend X energy/willpower/healing surges to squeeze themselves tighter into shadows and hold their breath, or they can make a physical stat + brawl or melee check to quietly knock out or kill the searcher. *[Or this failure can lead into a combat, if you like, but I have other fights coming up.]*

Once clear of the mob, the party can slink into the shadows at the edge of Dunspire. There are a few abandoned buildings below the high-water mark there. When the village was new, they must have underestimated the high Grandfather tide. Sections of town were washed out and abandoned. At this low tide, they're empty but more or less habitable.

The Dunspire villagers know about these buildings, of course, so they won't be safe for long. But the group's hiding place will last long enough for them to don their gear and catch their breath. And to realize that Danya didn't make it out.

[If the characters are paying attention during the crisis or specifically looking out for Danya, then I'll describe her lagging during the escape.

She balks jumping across a large gap between buildings, then is grabbed and dragged into the mob.]

The characters need to get Danya back if they can. If she's still alive... And there's the question of why the villagers would attack the outsiders. Do they attack all travelers like this? Or does it have something to do with their mission to find the Sign?

Church Picnic

Alak'ai doesn't know inlander ways, but this is his mission and he believes that there might be information about it in Dunspire. First they need a plan, though.

The characters can scout around with a physical stat + stealth roll (with energy, willpower, or healing surges paid as the price for failure) and find two pieces of good news. First, their horses are still at the inn. They're just too valuable to kill. The second result is that they can spot a mob of villagers dragging Danya – alive – into the Dunspire church.

Danya is inside the strange church of Zelletar, and if there's a chance of finding information about the Sign – or maybe the Sign itself – then it's probably in there. So how do they get inside without having to fight the whole village?

Option 1: Gate-Crashing

Fully armed and armored, the characters *may* decide to just rush the church, force the doors, and kill their way to Danya – and anything else that might be hidden in the church. Dunspire villagers are still searching for the outsiders, so they're spread out and the group can reach the town square unchallenged.

But there are still torch-bearing villagers milling around in front of the church and the player characters will have to deal with them before getting inside.

Combat map: Cobbled village square with a large church on one end.

Sanity damage: None. Dunspire and its people are creepy, but not enough to actually damage the mind.

NPC bonuses: Alak'ai provides a bonus attack to one character each round. No bonus from Danya, though. Not until our heroes get her back.

Special rules: None.

Angry townspeople stats: The Dunspire villagers can basically use the same stats and attacks as the local toughs from Ashmont, but these are fanatics. They don't run when injured, and fight to the death with cries of "I'a Cthulhu!" and "Ftaghn!" on their lips.

Option 2: The Art of Disguise

The PCs might try a more subtle approach, stealing clothing and trying to bluff their way into the Dunspire church. With villagers out searching, there are empty homes with clothes to steal. The characters can break in with a physical stat + lock-picking skill, then make a physical stat + stealth roll to get in unseen.

Failure will cost energy, willpower, or healing surges, depending upon game system. Or if it seems like a good time for a fight, failing the stealth check can mean running into a group of villagers using the stats above.

Cloaks and long coats are easy enough to find, and can at least partially conceal the characters' armor and identity. Walking past the Dunspire villagers in the town square, though, will require a social stat + subterfuge or deception skill check. And because these are people who know everyone else in their town, there's a rather large penalty.

Failure means being spotted as outsiders and attacked as above in option one. But if the characters succeed, they can walk right up to the church doors.

Option 3: Stealth

The Dunspire church is built right into the mountain and the front doors are the only way in. Sneaking through a side entrance isn't an option. A physical stat + stealth roll can get the group to the front doors, but there's only so much cover along the skirts of the square and none at all in front of the church, so there's a high penalty.

If the characters can create a distraction on the other side of the square or across town, they can eliminate the penalty to sneak up to the front doors.

[A single entrance narrows the options for getting into the church, but leaves it open for players to find some creative solution that I completely missed. If they do, I'm certain I can mix and match some version of these three options together into a viable series of dice rolls.]

The Inner Sanctum

The outer chamber of the church is just as the PCs saw it before, but there's no one inside. The doors to the inner sanctum can be picked (physical stat + lock-picking or similar skill check) or simply forced open with a strength roll.

Beyond stretches a hallway leading to the inner sanctum, but the walls are decorated with strange murals depicting winged crustaceans, flying polypus masses, conical creatures with pyramidal heads, and other horrible things. Certainly no comforting saintly images of Zelleny and Rhystar leading the Antoran people to safety or standing against the tidal wave.

The PCs must resist X sanity damage as they hurry through the hall, past smaller doors, toward the inner sanctum and the sound of chanting.

[I was going to put a magical barrier around the church, but decided against it because Tydalus is a low-magic setting. There won't be a mage character who could disarm it, so I decided to just move on to the rescue.]

I'll have some enemies use magic later, and everyone will pay the price in sanity.]

Inside the church sanctum, Danya stands before an altar in a white dress, swaying on her feet. Her eyes are blank and she doesn't seem aware of her surroundings. Danya mumbles nonsense words – or *are* they nonsense? – to the kneeling cultists gathered before the altar, some of which they pick up and chant back. The characters recognize the words *Tekeli-li* and try not to focus too much on the others.

Behind the altar is another sealed door. But it's small, like a safe.

Looming over it all is a massive statue of a creature, something hideous carved from the same green-black stone as the reef temple. The body is vaguely anthropomorphic and that's being generous. It's scaled and all of its gangling limbs end in clawed fingers. Long, narrow wings rise over humped shoulders and between them sits a lumpish head. Even in stone, the eyes are malevolent and the mass of tentacles concealing the mouth are engraved with a vitality that makes it seem as if they will writhe to life at any moment.

Just being in the same room as the massive idol causes X sanity damage. *[Only a moderate amount for now. The characters can't leave yet, and I'll hit them again as they have to spend time with this blasphemy carved in stone.]*

Combat map: Temple interior.

Sanity damage: Each combat round, the characters must resist X sanity damage from the statue looming over them. *[Small amount here, too, because it's going to hit every turn.]*

NPC bonuses: Alak'ai provides a bonus attack to one character each round. Danya's bonus still isn't available.

Special rules: With a physical stat + stealth check, the PCs can sneak up on the Dunspire cultists. Each character that succeeds in their stealth check gets a surprise round or bonus to initiative. But if they fail or decide to just charge, the cultists leap to their feet and unsheathe ritual daggers.

Cultist stats: The Dunspire cultists are even more fanatical than the village mob and are trained in murder, so they'll have tougher stats and attacks. I'll also give them a zealous attack that deals more damage the more they are hurt.

A high priest will lead them, and he'll attack with some actual magic, causing sanity damage as well as physical damage.

If any of these cultists are taken prisoner, they will be more than happy to rant at the characters, but a dying cultist can also gasp out a few threats. The Elder Sign cannot – *must* not – leave this temple. The powers that it holds at bay will not sleep forever. One day, they will awaken.

That should be enough to make sure that the players know the Elder Sign is here in the church.

Danya will stop mumbling her strange words after the fight, but will collapse when the characters rescue her. She's unharmed – at least physically – but being kidnapped and then brought into this profane temple hasn't done her already bruised mind any good.

The safe behind the altar has a keyhole and searching the priest turns up a matching key. If the characters take their time, they must also continue to resist sanity damage from the statue, just as they did during the fight.

Inside the tiny vault is a smooth stone. It's a little larger than the palm of a person's hand and carved with a wobbly-looking star – almost crude, as if etched by a child – and a single eye engraved in the center. But looking at it is somehow soothing and the character holding it stops taking sanity damage.

The characters have Danya and they have the Elder Sign. Now it's time to go and I suspect the group will be racing to leave before they lose their minds. In the hallway, at least, the toll on their sanity isn't constant and as long as they don't stop to study the murals in too much detail, they lose no more sanity.

You Are Now Leaving Dunspire

Getting out of the church is easy, but escaping Dunspire may be more difficult. There are hundreds of villagers and they can't all be killed, especially while the party is leading an insensate Danya. But one of the small rooms off the church hall – and the slain cultists inside the inner sanctum (if anyone wants to brave going back in there) – have robes and hoods. The party can disguise themselves as cultists, counting on their religious authority.

There are villagers outside, but a social stat + lying skill roll can bluff the characters' way past. If they don't use some disguises, they will have to use stealth or else fight their way through the villagers. *[Basically how they got into the church, but in reverse.]*

If the characters can just get to their horses, they will be able to ride out of Dunspire faster than the villagers can follow.

Chapter reward

The same as before, a reward of some experience for my players to spend. And then a health boost and combat skill increase that the player characters will need to survive the last chapter of my game.

CHAPTER 4

Pursuit

Chasing an ancient Kelanua song, the characters traveled to one of Vanhome's small, remote villages: Dunspire. They found a town full of cultists there, worshiping dark powers and the Elder Sign – a powerful weapon against horrors from beyond the stars – hidden away from humanity by those powers' servants. After retrieving the Elder Sign and rescuing Danya, the PCs have escaped Dunspire on horseback and left the zealous villagers far behind.

But the cultists of Dunspire are not defeated. They serve powers beyond human understanding and recklessly tap into them. With their captive and their sacred charge taken, they summon a creature from beyond the veil.

The summoning takes time, however, and the player characters do have the advantage of horses. They have a few days to travel and recover. Danya snaps out of her trance, but remains remote and troubled. Half of her speech is confused and she lapses often into other languages. Danya has only brief moments of lucidity, when she thanks her friends for rescuing her once again and apologizes for letting herself be captured.

Danya shies away from the Elder Sign, but she can actually help figure out how to use it. She knows that the cult couldn't destroy it, which is why they sealed it away and guarded it. She thinks that the Elder Sign could be taken back to the temple where she released the Tekeli, and they can use it to defeat the huge alien creature. The temple... amplifies forces.

Danya knows – or at least has a strange intuition – how to use the Sign, but can't order her thoughts on it. It's as if her mind or the Elder Sign itself resist it.

The following day, the cultist's summoned hound seeks out its unprepared prey. The player characters must make a mental stat + alertness check to notice a shape fluttering down from the twilight sky. To call the thing bird-like or bat-like, or even insectoid goes just partway toward forcibly bringing it into human definition. The only certain attribute that can be given to it is webbed limbs and membranous wings.

The Byakha – an alien beast tamed long ago by inhuman hands and whose flocks roam the unknown spaces until called – swoops down on the riding group. Danya shrugs and says that it's only ordinary matter, dismissing the creature as a threat.

Combat map: Mountain pass.

Sanity damage: Witnessing the Byakha deals X sanity damage. *[This one is a large hit. It's the final chapter of the game and time to really drive the horror home.]*

NPC bonuses: Alak'ai provides a bonus attack to one character each round. But Danya doesn't fight because she doesn't recognize the beast as a threat.

Special rules: None.

Byakha stats: Inspired by the Byakhee of the Cthulhu Mythos, Byakha are winged monsters which move too fast and at impossible angles that have nothing at all to do with their wings. It will dive and swoop, making fly-by attacks with a lot of movement attributes on them. I want the players to struggle a bit to corner the swiftly-moving Byakha, but if it proves too difficult to hit, I'll have Alak'ai pin it for a moment with his harpoon to give them a chance to deal some damage.

Once the Byakha is dead, the alien body will deal a little extra sanity damage unless the party rides or walks on. Quickly.

Return to The Nautilus

Now it's only a few more days to reach The Nautilus. The characters can resupply there and receive any healing that they haven't been able to provide for themselves, but Alak won't want to stay for long. The *Iron Eel* is docked at The Nautilus and as soon as they've caught their breath, Alak'ai will set sail. The PCs can do any more resting and catching up at sea.

The *Iron Eel* sails toward The Hunter once again and they have a week to make plans. At least one part of the plan is easy... Rather than returning to The Hunter, Alak'ai will sail further out to sea to bypass the Tekeli, circling behind it to reach the island. Danya says that's where the Elder Sign must be used to amplify its power.

But how can they use it...? One night during the voyage, Danya will approach whichever character she's become closest to. She's lucid today, and afraid. She understands how to use the Sign now, and it terrifies her. Danya tells her friend that the Elder Sign must be powered by a life.

Hopefully encouraged by her friend, Danya will speak to the others and explain that a sacrifice must be made in order to charge the Elder Sign with life force. A life given willingly.

To defeat the Tekeli, someone must die. Alak will let the characters talk, but won't force anyone to make any decisions. If there are any immediate volunteers to give up their lives, Alak will tell everyone to sleep on it.

[But I'm not going to have him offer one of the nameless crew as an option. It's Alak'ai's job to protect them, and besides, the sacrifice loses all drama if some unknown sailor makes it. If none of the players want to kill their characters, that's fine – that's why I've kept Alak and Danya around all this time.]

Race to the Temple

It takes a week to sail back toward The Hunter, but the characters can see the beacon light shining upward into a ceiling of gray-green clouds the entire voyage. A few days out, they spot the top of the tower itself and its lamp throwing out a beam of light.

[This is really more sequel time than we need, but I can't have the trip back down the coast take less time than the journey out. I might be able to shorten the sea voyage from The Nautilus back to The Hunter by placing wind and tides in the group's favor, but I'll probably abstract the trip. I have nothing in particular planned to fill the downtime, but the players may have something. I could fill the journey back with encounters more like the trip out, but we're heading for the climax of the story. I need to keep the game pace up and I want my players thinking about who's going to die to stop the Tekeli. I don't want to bog them down with a whole bunch of effectively meaningless combat. I have a few crises and combats at the end, but I intend to bunch them up into a single tense scene.]

But the sky has that ill-fated green cast, and soon the characters can see the other Kelanua ships and the black mass of the Tekeli again. They must resist X sanity damage once more, but soon they should be able to end this threat.

Alak orders the *Iron Eel* to head out into deeper waters, to circle around the Tekeli. But the gurgling liquid creature has some intelligence or instinct, and it oozes across the ocean after them.

The *Iron Eel* turns away from the Tekeli and though the gooey horror follows, it seems unable to approach closely. It sends some inky pseudopods questing outward, but the Kelanua sailors soon become adept at dodging the clumsy swipes.

The wind carries the Tekeli's garbled utterances and the player characters need to resist another hit of X sanity loss as the gurgling voice gibbers relentlessly. By dawn the following day, two of the *Iron Eel's* crew have slit their wrists in their bunk. Another sailor throws themselves overboard – only to be snatched out of the water by the Tekeli and dragged into one of its many mouths.

The Elder Sign isn't charged up from those deaths, Danya says. The stone requires a willing and deliberate death given to it.

As the ship draws finally closer to the island, the Tekeli ripples violently and surges after them. It seems desperate to stop the boat from reaching its destination.

Alak'ai shouts for more sail! It's now a race to reach the island before the Tekeli can cut them off. Everyone must make physical stat + athletics or boating checks to help the *Iron Eel* race ahead of the Tekeli. The characters need X number of successes.

If they fail, the Tekeli sends a pseudopod out to lash the *Iron Eel*. Its teeth scrape the hull and shake the ship, and everyone aboard takes X damage. *[This is only a moderate hit. We're in the endgame now, but there is combat ahead and I don't want the characters too beat up before it even begins.]*

The Tekeli recoils from the *Iron Eel*, though. It's the Elder Sign. Even dormant, it repels the creature, though the Tekeli is far from defeated. Wind howls out of the darkening sky and the sea grows rough. The Tekeli rears up, lifting a black blob out of the water, and then smashes it back down. Alak'ai shouts to brace for waves and the titanic splash tries to capsize the ship.

Everyone has to roll a physical stat + athletics skill check to keep their feet. Each PC that fails takes X amount of damage. *[Another mid-sized hit.]*

The Tekeli stretches a tendril past the ship, trying to bar their passage. Alak orders his crew to arm the deck catapults. The *Iron Eel* has a couple barrels of liquid fire and they had better use them. Alak'ai doesn't like their chances of sailing through the strand of Tekeli and they can't rely on the Elder Sign while it's unpowered.

The PCs can make mental stat + athletics skill rolls to work the catapults. *[Maybe some other skill will apply, if there's anything in your system suitable for siege weapons.]*

The player group needs X number of successes. For each point that they fall short, they must spend energy, willpower, or healing surges *[depending upon your RPG system]* to make up the difference and reach their target number.

If they still fail to hit the necessary level of success, the Tekeli plunges a fanged tendril into the water and attacks the ship's keel. The *Iron Eel* bucks and everyone aboard takes X damage. *[This one is a bigger hit because it's the result of subsequent failures – first of the roll, then to spend the necessary resources.]*

Alak'ai draws a deep breath and orders the crew to hold steady at full speed. If they slow at all, the Tekeli will get close enough to threaten the ship again.

So the *Iron Eel* hits the rocky shore of the island at full speed. Each PC must make a physical stat + athletics check as the ship crashes into the rocks. The bow splinters and the deck heaves, and every character takes X damage. If they succeeded their athletics check, then they only take half damage.

Alak'ai tells everyone to abandon ship, and he and the characters leap onto the shore. Danya flees the ship, running frantically inland. Other sailors – many of them wounded – drag themselves from the wreck. Behind them, the Tekeli heaves itself onto land to engulf the ship and the screaming crew. *[And conveniently killing off NPCs that might complicate things for me during the ending sacrifice.]*

All player characters must roll to resist X sanity damage from the grisly sight of the creature forming mouths and claws just to rend the people that they have sailed with for weeks into pieces.

The survivors clamber over the slick rocks toward the temple, but once again the crab-like Dekara rise from the pools to attack. The longer the characters spend fighting the Dekara, the closer the Tekeli comes.

Combat map: Rocky area with pools. *[I'll use the same map as I did during their first encounter. It's a nice mirror of Chapter 1... and saves me a little work.]*

Sanity damage: Each character must resist X sanity damage. *[I'll increase this a little from the first encounter as the Tekeli surges toward them from behind, gibbering and terrible.]*

NPC bonuses: Alak'ai provides a bonus attack to one character each round, and Danya lets one character re-roll a single attack or defense each round.

Special rules: The Tekeli gushes after them, too, and on round two, it begins hurling stones and each player character will have to dodge them or else take X damage. The faster they can end this, the safer they'll be.

Dekara stats: There are four Dekara for each player character. *[At the end-game power level, the group should be able to kill them a lot faster.]*

This is the last appearance of the crab-men! They have the same stats as before – big pinching attacks, some push, and a grapple – but the player characters are at their most powerful now. They can enjoy beating up some weaker enemies to make them feel better after being battered around by the crises.

The Frayed Ends of Sanity

The characters slaughter the Dekara and run from the encroaching Tekeli. It rips up and hurls barnacle-encrusted island stones, and flings broken Dekara corpses as it chases after them.

The temple looms up just ahead, standing strangely against the horizon. It's impossible to tell if the structure is leaning to the point of collapse or if it was always meant to look that way. The doors of the ancient temple still stand open, pushed wide by the Tekeli's escape, and the characters can sprint inside ahead of the monster's fury.

The walls and pillars inside of the temple are no longer coated with the dormant Tekeli and are now plain to see. It is built of the odd black-green stone that is the same color as Grandfather Moon.

Detailed frescoes and murals depict strange scenes and odd creatures. There's an image of a thing scaled like a fish or reptile, but so obscenely twisted that it's impossible to determine its body shape. Another image shows an endlessly looping mass of coils, scaled like snakes, but lined with suckers like a cephalopod. They wind back on themselves in such convolutions that the coils could belong to many creatures or to one with no head and no end.

Beneath the party's feet, the temple floor is set with a mosaic depicting the winged, tentacle-mouthed horror that the characters saw in the Dunspire church. Paintings surrounding these images show creatures offering terrible sacrifice and tribute, but even the worshiping figures are less human than the Dekara.

The worst part is the knowledge that these aren't merely images. They're carvings, true, but they're not just the product of an artist's imagination. These things are *real*. The characters know that now and must resist X amount of sanity damage. *[Big hit here. We're right on the threshold now.]*

But the characters all walk or stagger further into the temple. There's an altar made of the same stone as the rest of the building, stained black with the blood of untold sacrifices, and beyond the altar is a sunken area with a closed hatch leading down. Whatever this temple was, it's dedicated to something far more powerful and malevolent than the Tekeli. The liquid monster was only the scum on the surface of the pond, hiding far greater horrors in the depths below.

Break With Reality

If she's not already carrying the Elder Sign stone, Danya sidles up next to the character who is and lifts it. If she steals the Sign from one of the PCs, they may make a mental stat + alertness check to notice her taking it. For each point of success scored, they get a bonus to stop Danya from getting rid of it.

The frightened and tormented Strazni girl backs away, toward the temple doors. She rants that the elder gods will return and their waking will drown the world. Humans know *nothing*, and they don't own this planet. Their culling cannot be stopped!

Danya screams that she must throw the Elder Sign into the sea. The elder gods forbid its existence. Humans are unknown to the first gods, too small for notice, but resistance will bring their attention down on Tydalus. And that cannot be risked.

The player characters can shoot or cut Danya down, wrestle the Elder Sign out of her hands, or talk her out of her delusion (though how much of a delusion it is will be open to debate) with a variety of checks: social stat + social skill, physical stat + athletics to charge her, then a physical stat + combat skill to kill or subdue her.

[I'll have to play it by ear and this moment will be more role-played than rolled on dice.]

Sacrifices Must Be Made

The Tekeli surrounds the temple, slamming against the doors but is unable to pass. The Elder Sign keeps it at bay, but the monster is still a long way from being defeated. The characters all know that this temple can amplify certain forces and that with it, the Elder Sign could banish the Tekeli, but it requires a sacrifice. One of them has to die.

If Danya survived her betrayal, she begs to be the sacrifice. She is in pain and knows she can never be trusted again. She thanks her friends for all they have done, but Danya would rather die while she's still human. If the characters had to kill Danya, then Alak'ai will volunteer to die.

[But these are both just backup plans. Either Alak'ai or Danya will remain quiet if any player character wants to be the hero of this storyline. If it looks like any of the PCs are going to make the sacrifice, I'll ease up on Danya's final breakdown so it's not as much of a mercy to let her go.

*The point, however, is that the player characters are the stars of this
story, and they get first pick on heroic deaths.]*

The characters can perform the sacrifice however they want to,
but it's intent that matters. When the brave character dies, the Elder
Sign begins to burn with a clear blue light and the Tekeli screams
with all its myriad mouths. It shudders and convulses, shaking the
temple, but its cries fade into echoes. The Tekeli becomes translu-
cent, growing fainter as the Elder Sign glows brighter.

Within seconds, the Tekeli vanishes as if it never existed at all,
banished from this reality.

An End to Madness

The PCs can leave the temple now, hopefully never to look on those
blasphemous images again, or to witness what other strangeness
might emerge from the darkness within. Eventually, the ocean will
cover the reef and its temple once more.

Until the next low tide...

Ships followed the Tekeli and the *Iron Eel* – at a distance – to the
island. With the monster gone, they're now anchored just off-shore.
The Kelanua fleet can take the party back to The Hunter, but if the
characters wish, they may bombard the temple and bring it down,
hopefully sealing the lower chambers.

When they return to The Hunter – with two days' sailing to rest
and recover – they will be received by Keeper Lukoa. The mercenaries will be paid in enough salt to let them live comfortably for
the rest of their days in any of the Antoran cities.

No such riches for anyone that began as prisoners, but Lukoa
does give them their promised freedom and a little salt to pay their
way inland. And all of the characters are welcome to remain at The
Hunter for as long as they like. They have each earned respect and
acceptance here. And a home, should they want one overlooking
the sea.

[Endings are difficult. Lukoa will hand out the reward and make his offer, then I'll let the PCs make their decisions and play out any final scenes with each other or the NPCs.]

Chapter reward

There's no reward for the last chapter of the campaign. My story is finished and the character arcs are all done. Now it's time for my players to begin thinking about the *next* game, the next story, and their next characters.

CHARACTER CREATION

Tydalus is just about ready to run. I have the story all laid out, with dice rolls and rewards and combat maps. The next thing I'll need to do before the campaign begins is create characters with my players. The PCs are the stars and heroes of the story, so knowing about my players and the characters that they create will be important.

Erica

Erica is my wife of fourteen years and girlfriend for several before that, so we've gamed with one another a *lot*. We also write novels together, and I know we work well as a creative team.

Erica's a great role-player, too. We have similar dramatic vision, so that gives her a good feel for the direction that I'm trying to take a story and she usually helps me get there. Even when she's not my Costoryteller, Erica's focus during any game is to advance the story, create a personal and/or romantic arc for her character, and to enable the other PCs in their personal arcs.

Erica's what I usually call a *power player*. Not a power gamer, but a power *player*. She's not looking to roll up the most powerful character, but she always has ideas and is willing to speak up when the story calls for dialogue. When there's downtime, Erica always has something going on with her character, a project or a conversation to strike up with an NPC or another PC.

Players like Erica are an asset in any game because they hold the group together, help keep everyone focused on the story, and also encourage other players to develop their own stories. But...

There's a good and bad side to pretty much everything in life. And the downside to power players like Erica is that they tend to get twice as much "screen time" as other players. Erica can monopolize game time or jump into scenes where other characters want to take the lead, but were just a little slower to react. Sometimes other players can feel left out.

The good side is that I can devote more of my time and energy to drawing those other players into scenes and helping them participate. Erica doesn't take a lot of my energy – she brings her own. And when somebody can let Erica know that they want to get out in front, she's not just willing to take a step back, but will get behind the other players and push.

Erica is often highly invested in a romantic arc, just like in our novels. Maybe that's not your thing, but Erica's romantic arcs have given us some hilarious and dramatic gaming memories. She likes a tough story arc to her romances as well. Erica wants to have to fight for it, whether she's the one pursuing or being pursued. She tries to pace the arc of the romance to that of the story, so both reach their peak around the same time.

Erica usually prefers to play strong, intelligent characters, often with some kind of scholarly background. It comes in handy when she's my Costoryteller, because her characters have good in-game reasons to be familiar with the lore and setting. She helps provide info-dumps when the players encounter something new.

In this RPG, Erica is my Costoryteller. We're writing the Tydalus novels together, and so we did all of the world-building and outlining together, too. She already volunteered to sacrifice herself if none of the other PCs want to at the end of Chapter 4, but that was months ago now. By the time we finish our outlines and finally get everyone together to play, Erica usually forgets the finer details of the game and she's almost as in the dark as the rest of the group.

Unsurprisingly, Erica has opted to play a scholarly character in Tydalus. Everyone else was making hardcore fighters, so someone with social skills to get them out of trouble seemed like a good idea. She's also got the academic skills to help make sense of what the group runs into, but isn't much of a fighter. Her combat skills and attacks will be more support-based.

So Erica created Safi, a Massir girl from Miskaton, the city of scholars that I named after H.P. Lovecraft's Miskatonic University. Safi grew up in a house with more books than food and was happily on her way to becoming a scholar just like her parents – until her father's telescope was stolen. Safi tried to steal it back, but being more of an academic than a fantasy-world super-spy, Safi promptly got caught and sent to the salt mines on the coast.

Erica did have a concern, though. She likes to play those intelligent, academic characters and Safi started to feel like a repeat for her. She didn't want to abandon her concept – which she liked – but had to give it a bit of a twist. Erica usually likes to play heroic characters, but decided that all Safi cares about is getting home. She's going to use all of that intelligence and social skill to survive and get home to Miskaton as quickly as possible. Nothing else matters.

Playing a coward can be tricky, and Erica doesn't want to *actually* screw over any other characters to save her own. Fortunately, as a lighthouse prisoner, Safi's basically the property of the Kelanua until her sentence is done. Safi doesn't get to run away when things get scary, so Erica has a reason to remain with the group and participate. And as a coward, surrounding herself with skilled fighters is a smart idea and means that Safi has to stay on their good side.

That gave Erica a different flavor for Safi, and guided her during character creation. The system we're using lets the players create custom attacks for their characters, so Erica named hers *Survivor's Strike* (which has defensive bonuses that Safi will retain for herself until she befriends the group), *Keep Your Distance* (which lets Safi hit and then run away), and *You Do It* (an attack that gives another character a free strike).

Cedar

I've known Cedar almost as long as I've known my wife, so we've been friends for a long time. We actually met through gaming, so it's been a part of our relationship since we were quite young.

Cedar has a different role-playing style than Erica. Social scenes are her favorite part of game, so I often try to include parties and social gatherings, but Cedar's a fairly shy and passive player. She participates in scenes happily, but doesn't initiate many of them. During those scenes, Cedar tends to respond to conversation more than begin it, and I don't expect her to be the first to speak up.

Cedar's sweet and kind, and her characters are almost all care-takers. She plays healers and support characters, and gets a lot of satisfaction out of it. She's never role-played for the combat, so her characters are usually quite gentle. Cedar can certainly throw down when she has to, but she's also played characters with practically no combat skill. Not that she's never been outside of her comfort zone – Cedar memorably played a demoness in a game of mine who was a brutal, remorseless killer that kind of scared everyone else.

Cedar is usually invested in her romantic arcs, too. While Erica tends to stir the shit, though, Cedar's passive style puts the ball in my court more often than not. Cedar will typically get attached to the first NPC to show an interest in her and advancing the romance is usually up to me. But Cedar and Bryan (the next player on my list) are in a relationship now and they're trying out romantic arcs with their characters, which makes my job a lot easier. I don't need to worry about creating a romantic NPC and all those scenes are between the two of them. I lend a hand pacing the story arc here and there, but that's a lot less work.

For Tydalus, though – and to make me a liar – Cedar decided to play a mercenary hired out to bolster the forces of one of the light-houses. Based on the setting information, she liked the sound of a cold, hard, Strazni warrior. For all of the kind healers Cedar plays, being a cynical badass is cathartic and she felt like playing someone with a sharp wit and a sharper sword for this game. Which is great, because I wasn't planning on a lot of parties and social intrigue in a game of cosmic horror.

After discussing the world and setting, Cedar named her character *Zoja*, and decided she came from Vanhome, one of the more militaristic city-states. Vanhome's primary exports are arms, armor, and people who know how to use them. Zoja learned to fight from one of the schools there, then set out to sell her services. Protecting a lighthouse isn't glamorous, but the Kels pay in salt.

Cedar bought a lot of military training and combat skills, giving Zoja heavy armor, a shield, and a big sword.

No, wait... she just changed her mind and decided to go with dual axes.

Because axes.

But Zoja's attacks are still all about drawing and holding enemy attention, and then chopping their asses off. Zoja has one attack with some movement so she can bail if she bites off more than she can chew, or so she can charge in and start getting in trouble. That attack also gives an ally some movement, so she named it *Set 'Em Up*. Bryan named one of his attacks *Take 'Em Down*, since they're playing partners.

Zoja's built to tank for the group, with the best armor and lots of health, but she has some decent damage output, too. Because axes.

Cedar found some character art she liked and in the picture, the woman has pale eyes. So she went ahead and took a disadvantage for that because the Kelanua distrust blue and green eyes and most of this game is going to be on the *Iron Eel*. Zoja's sea-eyes will make for some interesting play. I won't have the first Kel that Zoja meets try to drown her because her eyes are blue, but I'll make her life a little harder.

Insert sinister Storytelling cackle here.

Bryan

I've been friends with Bryan for a dozen years, so I know him well, too. Bryan's an IT guy, interested in computers and video games. He didn't play a lot of make-believe when he was a kid, so he's a little more literal-minded in his role-playing and tends to freeze up if I engage his characters socially. Bryan's had some very memorable scenes and some damn fine role-playing, but most of the time, he's one of my quieter players.

Bryan doesn't mind the social scenes, though, and he likes the combat just fine. But what Bryan likes best is a project to invest in. He wants to build or create something that involves a number of long, extended rolls. Bryan ends up playing a lot of artificers, engineers, and wizards. When I can, I try to build some kind of project into the game for him. But just as often, he comes up with something of his own on the side. As long as there's room for it in the game, he's happy.

Bryan also recently discovered that he likes tanking in battle. (In case you're not familiar with the term, *tanking* means getting into the enemy's face and taking as much of the damage as possible to protect the squishier characters.) Bryan is practically giddy when he can take some damage meant for another character, and likes to keep track of how many times he gets beaten into unconsciousness. Seriously, he gets a little disappointed if he never gets beat down. I try to make sure that at least a few crises have opportunities for Bryan to soak up some damage for someone else, and I lean on him a little harder in combat because he's a masochist.

But Bryan is a bit decision-impaired. Give him two choices and he will have a *very* hard time deciding between them. Three choices doubles his thinking time. If you let him, Bryan will just roll a die to decide what to do. Maybe that works for some people, but randomness isn't something we like to introduce to character development. Characters should have growth arcs, not zig-zags that fold back on themselves and wind up way out in left field. At least, not in novels or movies, and that's the kind of experience I'm trying to capture in my role-playing games.

I try to give Bryan very straight-forward decisions, with obvious right or wrong answers, if only so we don't have a ten-minute break for him to make up his mind. During character creation, he usually needs a lot of guidance. There are too many choices and Bryan can get really bogged down.

Helping him out turned into suggesting specific builds because I know him and know what he likes to play. Then Bryan just asked me to make his characters for him. Once he has a character that he can spend his experience points into and play the game with, he's set. Bryan's even asked me to provide his character concept a few times. I know the game world better than he does, so Bryan trusts me to give him a concept that he will enjoy. No pressure.

That's not something I've done for anyone else, or can imagine doing for any other player. But since he started having me make his characters, Bryan's considerably more relaxed going into game and he's enjoyed all of my creations. As long as it works for him, it works for me.

Making Bryan's characters for him demands a little work on my part, but I can have fun with it, too. I make suggestions that I know will cause interesting scenes in the game or that give me places to screw him over later in a way that will be interesting to watch.

So I went into character creation for Tydalus with a couple of ideas for Bryan. Cedar had mentioned that she was going to play a mercenary, so I thought I might make Bryan her partner. Because of how he usually likes to play, I had one idea for a big guy, with big armor, and a big weapon that he had an almost romantic relationship with. A big sword as a romantic rival for Cedar seemed like it would have some comedic mileage.

But Tydalus isn't exactly a lighthearted setting, so I asked Bryan if he wanted to try playing someone darker and more serious than his usual fare. I pitched a backstory where a teenager living in poverty kills the debt collectors sent to take what little his family has left. Fortunately, the crime boss recognized the talent it took to kill his collectors and offered Bryan's character a job to pay back the debt – as an assassin.

Bryan loved the idea. Apparently enough that while I was busy working with Erica, Cedar, and Jack (the last player in this game and next on the list), Bryan took off running, choosing attributes and making his character instead of having us do it. No paralyzing indecision at all. Interestingly, his assassin didn't end up a damage-sponge at all. I guess someone else is going to take a pounding in all those crises I made. My money's on Zoja.

Bryan named his character *Gavril*, in another uncharacteristic bout of swift decision-making. Usually naming his character takes weeks. I'll take this as a good sign.

Bryan made an Antoran (meaning no strong Strazni, Bhataari or Massir lineage) assassin with a lot of stealth skills and poisoned throwing knives so that he could fight either up-close or at range. Given that Bryan likes projects, I wouldn't be surprised if he asks me if he can create a new toxin, or maybe use his poison-making skills to craft other drugs – probably the kind that characters can use to cope with insanity.

The guy is definitely already up to something. During character creation, Bryan raised his hand and said, "Your equipment list says knives are common enough that I can start with them for free. Just how many knives are free?"

I had to make a quick call on that and offered him a low price for each batch of five knives. So Bryan wanted to know if fifteen blades counted as being *covered* in knives.

Gavril's attacks include a poison to weaken enemies and impose status effects that his assassin training can then turn into damage. And he had matched some of his attacks to Cedar's – *Set 'Em Up* and *Take 'Em Down* – so they complement each other well.

Since Gavril's an assassin and Zoja's a mercenary, I asked what they thought of a backstory where Bryan's character had been hired to kill a person that Cedar's was being paid to protect. As the start of a partnership, it sounded enjoyable and both players loved the idea. I asked them which one of them ended up doing their job – the assassin or the bodyguard. They thought it over and decided that each time they told the story, it ends differently.

That made for a fun quirk and doesn't really impact the ancient temple I'm going to pit them against, so I signed off on the idea.

I also asked Cedar and Bryan if they wanted to play a romantic arc between their badass mercenaries. They both shrugged, saying that they probably wouldn't. When I asked Cedar if I should send an NPC romance her way, she declined.

Everybody is throwing me curveballs this game. No problem, I think that I can roll with them. I may be mixing my metaphors, but an important part of Storytelling is remaining flexible and working with what your players give you.

Within reason.

Jack

I've only gamed with Jack once, and at the time, I didn't know what to expect. I'd invited another friend – Beth – to join my group for a game. Beth wanted to bring Jack and it was a package deal, so I said sure. I didn't want to be too hard on a new player, so I didn't push or control Jack real hard during character creation.

And I paid for it. Jack gave me a vague concept for an assassin with a background on the streets and didn't even give me that much until the day we started the campaign. He didn't give me much of a personality for his character either, so I had some surprises when we started playing. It wasn't a show-stopper, and I adjusted to his quirky young assassin. He ended up fitting in well enough with the player characters, but I had to feel it out as I went.

Case in point: I like to weave personal stories into my main plot, so I came up with a side chapter for that game where the PC group visited his character's home city. I made a gang that he used to kill for who wanted revenge on the character for leaving. But then, long before reaching that point in the story, Jack told the whole group – in character – that he worked for a secret order of assassins that hunted enemies of his country.

Umm... Jack never ran that idea past me, actually, so this was the first I heard of it. Was it a bad idea? No, but Jack and I didn't get to talk it out and fit his idea into the larger world that I had created. I struggled to tie this sudden backstory into my game.

Fortunately, that story had a lot of political turmoil. After some thought, I came up with a rogue general who recruited assassins to kill targets that the government couldn't touch for political reasons. I even managed to link it to the general in command of one of the other player characters to connect the two of them.

I was able to give Jack the secret organization he imagined, and fit it into my setting. It all played out pretty well, but I wished that we had that conversation during character creation instead of half-way through game.

I was also worried that Jack and Beth would only talk to and befriend each other's characters, but they both surprised me. Jack actually bonded with Erica's character in that game, taking her on as a little sister. He was her friend, gave her advice, protected her in combat, and even helped to conceal her romance with one of the antagonists. Jack pursued a romantic arc of his own with an NPC and was engaged with the main plot. It all came together wonder-fully and Jack brought a lot to the game.

So even though Beth was busy, I was happy to invite Jack back for Tydalus. But I was determined to be more involved in his char-acter creation this time.

After I told the group about the world of Tydalus – which was an abridged version of the world-building chapter – Jack decided to play a Kelanua scout. He showed me some art that he had in mind, which was varying degrees of inappropriate for the setting, but then found something he liked even more and which better matched the look and feel of Tydalus.

I wrote up some stats for harpoons, which I thought would be a common weapon among the Kelanua and Jack chose to use one, jumping into the culture. I helped him choose some attributes that would complement the harpoon bonuses, mixing up some close-range and throwing attacks – including *Dreamcap's Sting*, which is a painful attack that penalizes the target on a hit. Jack named it after the psychotropic jellyfish that the Kelanua harvest. Kudos for the in-world reference and I was impressed at just how quickly Jack was getting into the world.

Jack named his character *Kaikoa* and decided that he probably ranges up and down the coast to inspect coves and things that wash up, and occupies the gull's nest on ships as a lookout. Jack went with alertness and investigation for scouting skills, with boating, nature, and navigation for sea-based skills. Which I'm thankful for, because the group is screwed if they don't have someone to carry them through all those boating crises.

Jack took some healing skills, too, and decided Kaikoa was the grandson of the lighthouse apothecary – which he ran by me. Jack also said that while Kaikoa can speak Antoran, he seldom does. He likes to sass people in Kelanua behind their backs. Given that the other character Jack played in my group was a snarky little assassin, I think I'm getting a good feel for the kinds of characters that he likes. There's going to be some trouble, and we'll see how long the sarcasm keeps up when the horrors of the abyss boil forth.

Jack also decided to give Kaikoa a trained seabird as a pet, something to carry messages. He named the bird *Popoki*, and an animal friendship ability will let Kaikoa benefit from his pet's bonuses – namely its enhanced vision. Tydalus is a low-magic RPG setting, so Kaikoa can't see through the bird's eyes or anything quite like that, but he knows Popoki well enough to distinguish a warning chirp from a *something interesting* squawk. Jack gave Popoki some NPC bonuses to help out in combat, too. The NPC bonuses make Popoki useful in a fight, but Jack doesn't have to manage a whole second character sheet for it.

FINISHING TOUCHES

Now that I know who I'll be tormenting in the world of Tydalus and we've set a date for our first session, it's clear that I have a little more work to do before game begins.

For one thing, I have to detail a little more of Tydalus than just the Kelanua lighthouses and the city of Vanhome. Erica wants to know where Miskaton is. What city did Gavril come from? I'll need more than a sketched-up napkin to wave at my players.

Behold the mapkin 2.0!

We had to come up with a lot more names.

Erica scanned our mapkin into a graphics program and traced it as a base. We roughed out some fault lines, because the movement of tectonic plates and volcanic pressures are what form mountains and that could give us a guide for some realistic-looking ranges. We wanted a whole lot of mountains, so we decided Korvath is where three tectonic plates meet. Erica placed all our mountains accordingly and we had our basic topography.

I had Erica nudge Sulaweya south so that there was a bit more ocean between the Kelanua's original home and Korvath. When the Antorans came across the land bridge, retreating to Sulaweya wasn't an option. I didn't want the Kelanua sailing home and messing up our history.

Next, we placed all of the Antoran city-states around the various mountain peaks and then lined the Kelanua lighthouses up and down the coast. I had originally imagined them all west-facing, but thirteen lighthouses apparently covers a lot of map, so we ended up with one or two fairly northern ones and the last lighthouse *way* down in the south, pretty much facing east. Let's just say that the Kelanua *really* didn't want the Cthyans coming back.

Each Antoran city-state is supposed to support one of the lighthouses, so we could finally pair them up on our map. It wouldn't make much sense for Innsmont (named after Innsmouth) to be the patron of The Nautilus, would it? But Innsmont as the patron city of The Leaping Fish lighthouse? That not only works geographically, but thematically. The Innsmouth of the Lovecraft Mythos is more or less where the fish-men do their thing. We didn't even plan for Innsmont and the Leaping Fish to line up – it just sort of worked out that way.

I love it when stuff fits so well by accident that my players will think I did it on purpose.

We also modified the map to extend Antora up into the north because the old Strazni lands there were supposed to stretch out under the aurora.

Not that it matters, really, because Antora sank beneath the sea long ago. But now all that stuff we made up about the Strazni and the northern lights makes sense.

After some discussion, Erica put Miskaton near Arkhome, and we named the shadiest city of Korvath *Falspire*. That's where Gavril grew up and where Safi tried to steal back her father's telescope.

Hmm... The Kelanua lighthouse attached to Falspire is The Eye, so that's where Safi would have been sent. I'll have to transfer her up to The Hunter, but that's alright. I can have her arrive at the new lighthouse on the first day of game.

Any other last-minute changes? Yes, actually.

I've decided to throw in some new short scenes for each of the players to get into character. A bandit attack for Gavril and Zoja to fight off on their way to employment along the coast, a scouting mission for Kaikoa where he finds something horrible washed up on shore, and Safi has to survive her first day at The Hunter, mining salt and talking her way out of getting beat up by other prisoners.

That should make for a nice customized beginning to the game, a chance to draw each of the players into the world of Tydalus and their own characters.

RUNNING THE GAME

After some last-minute polish and a few tweaks, it's finally time to run my campaign. This section is a session-by-session breakdown of how the game played out, with all the last-minute changes, stuff I pulled out of my ass as we went, curveballs the PCs threw my way, and more. Everything up until now was how I plan and create my game, but now you can watch as I follow that outline, trying to keep my players moving and course-correcting when I screw up.

Before we dive in, let's review a few names. I've got four players, each with their own character. I need to distinguish the actions of the player – *Jack rolled his dice* – from the resulting actions of the character – *Kaikoa climbed the rope*. That's eight names to keep track of, so here's a quick reminder who is playing who in Tydalus:

- **Erica** is playing **Safi**, the scholarly coward.
- **Cedar** is playing **Zoja**, the axe-wielding mercenary.
- **Bryan** is playing **Gavril**, the mercenary assassin.
- **Jack** is playing **Kaikoa**, the Kelanua scout.

There's nothing left now but to do this thing. Wish me luck!

CHAPTER 1

Low Tide

Session 1!

The game opening went pretty much as described back in the Chapter 1 outline – just some scene-setting and world-building. I was feeling pretty rusty, though. Between writing this book for you, and the holidays, and then some of my players getting sick, it's been months since we gamed. I introduced Captain Nakhona and he had some brief dialogue with Zoja and Gavril – Cedar and Bryan's pair of mercenaries – but it wasn't my best.

Still, we're all just getting started and I only needed to warm up. Cedar asked the captain what sort of combat they expected on the ship, since Zoja and Gavril have never worked for the Kels before. I used that to segue into a flashback one week ago, placing Zoja and Gavril on the road to The Hunter for lack of any wars between the Antoran cities to fight.

Highway Robbery

This flashback scene is one of the things I added during the final polishing phase. I wanted to give the chance for each player to show what their character does in their "natural setting." For Zoja and Gavril, their natural setting is brutally slaughtering people.

I described the mercenaries a week before, having picked up a job protecting a small caravan on its way out to the lighthouse with supplies from The Hunter's Antoran patron city, Dyrah. It gave me the chance to do a bit of scene-setting, describing how the low tide had opened up lower mountain passes that made good shortcuts – and that bandits had already staked their claim.

From there, I jumped right into combat. In hindsight, I should have had an NPC merchant in the caravan talk to Zoja and Gavril a bit, maybe ask their credentials or something to give them a chance to talk about their characters more. But like I said, I was feeling rusty and slow, and it was the first fifteen minutes of game.

But Cedar and Bryan seemed fine plunging straight into a fight. Bryan tried out Gavril's attacks, but Cedar seemed surprised to find out that her axe-centric combat build dealt so much damage. The bandits were individually pretty easy, meant to be fought as a large group, and Zoja mowed right through them – which led to some laughter from the group.

Bryan: "Zoja slices, dices, makes Julienne fries!"

Erica, pretending to be one of the bandits: "How did you know my name was Julienne?"

Bryan and Cedar seemed pretty happy with their characters and they made short work of all the bandits. I could have had a second wave emerge from cover and attack to extend the fight, but I wanted to get to the main story and the other players were waiting to come onto the scene.

The scene accomplished what I wanted, though – letting Bryan and Cedar practice fighting as partners (setting up flanking positions and such), and to let me test out what they could do. Based on their damage output, I'm going to need to either make tougher enemies, or throw a few more into the fray.

First Day

I switched back to present day, shifting focus to Erica's character, Safi. I had one of her fellow prisoners lean over and whisper to her, expressing her curiosity about the mercenaries. That was Danya, my biggest plot-related NPC and one of the primary antagonists. I didn't get to give any of Danya's backstory, but Safi did get to tell some of hers.

Which let me segue to another flashback! Safi was halfway through her prison sentence, and determined to survive the other half. When she had been arrested in Falspire, she was sentenced to five years at another Kelanua lighthouse, The Eye. There, Safi had talked her way out of the mines and into stores, using her education to get a better job. And working in stores gave Safi the opportunity to skim some salt and other supplies, then trade them to other prisoners in return for not shanking her at night. Everybody wins.

But this flashback scene began with the Keeper of the Salt – the lighthouse's quartermaster – deciding that The Eye had too many prisoners and not enough supplies to feed them all. They rounded up some of the Antorans to send to another lighthouse – including Safi. I only briefly described the send-off because I wanted to move on to introducing Safi's new home, The Hunter.

At The Hunter, a Kelanua warden ushered their new prisoners toward the salt-crusted cliffs. Safi started begging right away not to mine salt, pitching herself as a great worker inside the safety of the lighthouse. Erica's first persuasive rolls didn't go so well, but that's fine. I would have arranged for her to end up on the cliffs anyway.

Safi was sent to harvest salt from the rocks and a large, scarred, tattooed prisoner grabbed the best rope harness, leaving a frayed and tar-stained tangle for Safi. Erica was quick to try to better Safi's lot again, telling the larger prisoner that his harness was much too small. This time her persuasive roll went much better, and the big guy exchanged harnesses with her.

As the big guy walked toward the cliff's edge, I narrated another fiber snapping in the frayed ropes. Safi muttered that she hoped the other prisoner was sentenced here for killing a baby or something else awful enough to deserve this fate. Safi wants to survive her sentence, but she's not *entirely* cold-blooded.

Washed Up

Back to the present again, on board the *Iron Eel*. There, Captain Nakhona continued his rounds – trailed by the first mate, Alak'ai – and stopped to talk to Jack's character, Kaikoa. He told their young scout to keep his eyes open and maybe they would find where that strange stone came from, if anywhere at all.

What strange stone, you ask? Flashback!

I set a scene of Kaikoa ranging down the coast – though I didn't do a very good job and Jack missed that it was a flashback. Need to brush up on my flashback technique, I guess. But Jack's also a more inexperienced gamer, so I let him know that this was several days ago and Jack caught up quickly.

Kaikoa's bird, Popoki, was screeching and circling something in the distance. A scout's job is ordinarily to search for runaway Antoran prisoners and make sure no illegal salt-miners are chiseling wealth from the cliffs, but they also have to keep their eyes open for anything strange from the sea.

And Popoki had spotted something strange. Something washed up on shore... a large fish or whale, though it was lacking in recognizable fins and even more disturbingly, what limbs it possessed were far less familiar. Thankfully, the creature was dead and only half of a corpse was caught on the jagged rocks at the shore. But if that was any comfort, the monster bore teeth-marks from something even larger and less wholesome.

Jack was excited. He had never read any Lovecraft or played any Mythos-inspired games. Based on what I know of his taste in media, horror's not really at the top of his list, anyway. So while the other players were shuddering, Jack wanted Kaikoa to take one of the monster's fangs.

Okay, monster fangs are cool. Go for it, man.

...And then he wanted to cut off a piece of its rubbery flesh.

Uh, alright then. Moving hastily along.

The dead creature clutched something in one of its... hands? It was a chunk of broken stone, greenish-black and marked with lines that no kind of oceanic erosion might leave. But if that was writing, it was in no language that Kaikoa had ever seen. So Jack happily hacked off fingers until he could take the stone, too.

Well, Jack's decided that Kaikoa collects things, but he did say that he would show the stone to his commander. I told Jack it was passed to the Keeper of Ships (who is in charge of the boats, sailors, and scouts), and then all the way up to the Keeper of the Tower (the overall commander of a lighthouse).

Attacked at Sea

Back to the present one last time. I summarized that the *Iron Eel's* mission was to find the source of this strange stone, which I thought would be a cooler lead-in than a fishing trip. The island still gets to be a surprise to the players, though they know they're looking for something disturbing.

I made the old sailor, Hoka, Kaikoa's uncle and then started the next scene with Hoka's warning that something was coming. Jack didn't really seem to know what to do with this information, but I had Alak'ai take note.

And then I busted out the tentacles. Based on Zoja and Gavril's murderiness during their flashback scene, I increased the attack from eight to twelve tokens and everyone reacted with revulsion to tentacles with eyes instead of suckers. Except Jack. If you guessed that Kaikoa wanted to harvest one of the eyes, then you share his sick mind. Congratulations!

The fight went well and we got to see Kaikoa and Safi in action this time around. The harpoon-related abilities we built into Kaikoa worked pretty damned well, and in a contest for who can beat up more bad-guys in a fight, I think he'll give Zoja a run for her money.

It probably depends upon if the enemies cluster up for Zoja's axes or not.

Safi's *You Do It* attack also worked quite well. The other three characters each have special abilities that augment their weapon damage, even on basic attacks. Safi ran around using her ability to trigger attacks for the others, and they got to throw down nicely on her dime.

I ran into a snag during the fight, though. The tentacle that had snatched the man Safi was chained to also snapped her bonds so I could let her fight. But I had left Danya chained, and on round two, another monster tentacle grabbed her. I let the players know that they had only a round to save Danya before she was dragged down into the water.

And the characters just kept on taking shots at their own chosen targets. None of them had bonded with Danya or had the heroic personalities that would save her just on principle. For a moment, I had to consider that they might just let Danya be dragged into the ocean and I would lose this NPC. But I still had Alak'ai, my backup NPC, and I figured that I could have him be the one who goes mad if I had to. He's not as sympathetic as Danya, but I could make do.

Thankfully though, Erica was on the ball. She briefly narrated Safi feeling guilty for leaving a fellow prisoner bound and helpless, then turned back to poke the tentacle that had grabbed Danya and shouted for someone else to chop it off. But Erica got a critical hit, so even though Safi doesn't do near enough damage to actually free Danya in one blow, I gave it to her.

Bryan and Cedar decided that they were getting paid to protect this ship and helped out a little belatedly, but thankfully, I got to keep Danya. Who knows, though? She could die later and perhaps I'll have to come up with something else.

The fight went smoothly and even with the extra tentacles, no one got too badly beat up. But they did take some damage and they lost some sanity, which was what I wanted. The characters aren't going to have the time to heal up all the way before the next fight or crisis, so I don't want them too roughed up yet. I need them on their feet to smack around later.

And yes, Jack *did* have Kaikoa pluck an eye out from one of the tentacles. He was seriously more concerned with taking his trophy than fighting. After the battle, Jack decided that Kaikoa would give the eye to Alak'ai as a gift. Thanks for his NPC bonus? I don't know. He just told Alak, "Here, this is for you."

You do you, Jack... But this is a game of horror, so I had Kaikoa resist some sanity damage because a monster eye is a really messed up present. Alak'ai muttered something about handing it over to the lighthouse apothecary for study and then wiped his hands.

Riders on the Storm

The storm crisis went well and was fairly straightforward. Everybody jumped right into it. When the yard arm was going to sweep Alak overboard, Bryan asked what the roll was to help. I shrugged and said it depends on what he does. Cedar asked if there were ropes on the yard arm to grab and I said of course, so Zoja and Gavril threw themselves on a rope, holding the yard arm back while Kaikoa went up the rigging and tied it off.

I don't think my players failed a single roll in the crisis, but that's okay. Not every fight or crisis has to hurt the characters and more importantly, I gave them enough space in the crisis to come up with their own solutions – that wound up using the rolls I already had prepared – which is how it should be.

So far, so good.

Shipwrecked

The characters all rode out the storm, but there was nothing they could do about the rocks beneath the water. I dropped the curtain, faded to black, and then started them off waking up in the wreck. Since they did spend a night unconscious, I let them recover some health, energy, and sanity, though I gave it to them at reduced rates because instead of resting in a bed, they were sleeping face-down on a stony beach in soggy armor.

The characters pulled themselves up out of the water and took stock. There were the expected questions about where they were. I got to hand out some navigation checks and Kaikoa was the first to realize this place wasn't on any maps. Jack immediately volunteered to scout out the island. Which is great because Kaikoa's a scout. It sucks when someone is playing a baker and they never even try to bake anything, but I've got a good group of gamers who are all invested in their concepts.

Alak'ai was already organizing the Antoran prisoners and crew to pull the *Iron Eel* up onto shore. Always eager to get out of difficult or dangerous work, Safi sold herself as a cartographer, then offered to help Kaikoa map the island.

Then Erica did one of the things she does best – she drew other players in. She asked Alak'ai for some axes. He told her that there was no way they were giving a prisoner weapons – though Alak did hand her a broken oar to use as a staff – but Safi said that was fine. She would rather have an axe-wielding mercenary.

Just to split the party – because splitting the party makes players nervous and I *want* my players nervous – I had Alak authorize one mercenary to go with them. It also gave Zoja and Gavril a chance to have some dialogue. Cedar gave Zoja a thick accent, because she's deeply Strazni, and a cynical wit. She said Gavril owed her for the time he spent dancing with that tentacle.

"That wasn't dancing," he said. "It was trying to crush me!"

Zoja smirked. "Dancing, crushing. It is same thing."

I think that I can see what kind of relationship Zoja and Gavril have. But they sent Zoja, leaving Gavril to stay with the ship, and the scouting party ventured out.

The Call of Cthulhu

I didn't let the scouts get very far away, though, before everyone felt the eerie magical call of the temple. All my players groaned when I asked for an awareness check – different than alertness, and a skill that wasn't even on the list during character creation. Awareness is used to perceive things beyond the traditional senses, so there's no reason for anyone to have it.

Yet.

Despite the lack of awareness to help, everyone did okay on the first roll and earned the bonus to resist the call. But only Safi and Kaikoa actually succeeded there. Gavril and Zoja started to zombie-shuffle off further into the island while Erica and Jack had to roll to slow them down and tie them up until it passed.

Search & Rescue

The group recovered after a while and some rolls, wondering what the hell was going on, and I gave them a check to notice that Danya was gone.

Captain Nakhona argued to let her go, just like in my notes. But the PCs quickly argued to rescue Danya, so Alak'ai and Hoka didn't have to add much. Cedar even had Zoja ask if letting Danya wander off had anything to do with her eyes. Danya has blue eyes, which the Kelanua call *sea-eyes* and believe are a mark of strangeness, if not evil. Cedar gave Zoja sea eyes too, so I guess she ran with that to make a little bond. Perfect.

Nakhona grudgingly agreed to mount a rescue, but they set out in force: the player characters, Nakhona, Alak, wise old Hoka, and a few NPC mercenaries and sailors for me to slaughter later on.

They spotted Danya and the temple, but the dice were not kind to the players in resisting the sanity damage. That finally got the characters to use the booze in their equipment, which granted them a bonus in resisting sanity damage. They were all looking pretty mentally beat up. Even if I don't get to give out any derangement soon, I think that Gavril and/or Zoja might pick up an addiction.

Next, they ran into the Dekara. Zoja and Gavril did wonderfully in combat once again, dishing out damage and avoiding it for the most part, but got hit right in the sanity. One of them will definitely be the first to win a derangement. Kaikoa and Safi are higher sanity characters, but I managed to bloody them in the fight, so that's just another way of making them work for it.

And that's where we ended the first session. Cedar hadn't slept well the night before and was beginning to lose focus. We were all hungry and ready to break for dinner, anyway.

But everybody got to feel out their characters and try them in combat, and I established the kind of horror that they will face. My players are already groaning at alertness checks because they know that their characters will see something mind-torturing, which is right where I want them. Except maybe Jack, who might run gleefully down a morbid road to madness. We'll see where that goes.

I blew some rust off this time, and next session, I'll shore up my scene descriptions and transitions. I want to make sure to give the characters a little more time for dialogue, too. They got thrown in the deep end quickly this first session, but I think I can let them tread water a little now.

This game is going to have me thinking in watery metaphors for months.

Temple of Doom

Session 2.

The first session of the campaign was a little rough on my part. I wasn't happy with my descriptions and my segues required some work. It was also pretty hectic, with a lot of crises and combat, and not much time for anything else.

So for the second session, I decided to start with a sequel – that literary pause – so my players could catch their breath and get into character before I herded them right to the next plot point.

I started things off with a description of the scene of slaughter where they fought the Dekara (though they don't know that name yet). Then I said the first sound to break the silence after the battle was a man retching. I had Alak'ai throw up all over the beach and ask what the hell those things were.

Alak's an NPC, so it's a good idea to make sure that he's not too much of a badass. The PCs are the stars of this story, not the non-player characters. And since I've made Alak be generally competent so far, having him react with horror lets the players know that this is not normal, this is scary, and they might want to consider being frightened, too.

Kaikoa decided to examine the Dekara bodies, not quite unexpectedly. I let him poke around the battlefield, but then hit Kaikoa with some sanity damage because these things aren't built like humans. Making sense of their strange organs and guts is hard on the mind. And it's kind of creepy to stick your arm up to the shoulder into a dead monster.

I also had Kaikoa find a satchel woven out of kelp, hinting that these things are not mindless monsters, but tool-using and intelligent creatures. Hopefully, this makes them even more disturbing. Jack just seemed excited to examine the bag, but everyone else was properly creeped out.

So I gave Kaikoa a seaweed bag. I could have filled it with some random shit and made that the end of it, but that would be a bit of a dick move. I had Kaikoa take sanity damage in order to investigate, so the least I can do is make it worthwhile.

It was an excuse to do something interesting. I messaged Erica from my laptop and we briefly discussed what Kaikoa would find in the Dekara's red kelp bag, then settled on a mollusk that secretes a healing venom. It heals damage, but inflicts a little sanity damage.

The more damage that the shell heals, the higher the penalty to resist the sanity loss, though the amount stays small. Otherwise, the players would never use it.

I narrated Kaikoa noticing the little creature in the shell and Jack promptly had his character poke it. So he got some healing and lost some sanity, and learned how it works. Let's hope that thing gets lots of use throughout game.

But the PC group wanted to keep moving. Good, because Danya had wandered off while they fought the Dekara. They hurried to the temple and everyone but Jack cringed at the twisted, inhuman architecture. The doors were cracked open and Danya had gone inside. Erica wanted Safi to examine the doors to see if they opened frequently. She was curious to know if the crab-things used this temple. Investigation roll and... critical failure!

So Safi brushed away some algae clinging to the doors and uncovered a series of strange markings, much like the ones on Kaikoa's stone. Erica made sure that smart little Safi spoke every language on Korvath (Antoran, Strazni, Bhataari, Massir, and even Kelanua), but it wasn't any of those, and she took some sanity damage instead.

Nobody was excited to go into the temple and not even Kaikoa was jumping through the open doors. Safi called for Danya, which further did not excite Kaikoa. The young Kelanua had formed some professional pride as a stealthy scout and did *not* approve of the shouting. But when Danya didn't come running, they had to go in.

The NPCs lit some torches and both Erica and Cedar quickly volunteered to carry the light. Both Gavril and Kaikoa declined, of course, being the sneaky types, but Erica and Cedar know that fire is often the best bet against monsters. I explained that with a torch in one hand, Safi couldn't use her staff – which was really just a broken oar because the Massir scholar isn't exactly a warrior – and Zoja can't dual-wield her axes. Erica preferred a torch as a weapon, and Cedar had no problem at all switching to axe and torch for her two-weapon fighting.

Zoja said she wasn't coming back to this island without a whole company of Vanhome mercenaries and enough pitch to burn the temple down.

That's the spirit! She's wrong, of course, but it's still the right spirit.

I described the interior of the temple as creepily as I could, with poor Danya shivering in the darkness. Gavril and Kaikoa prowled out to grab her and Safi tried to talk to the other girl – so they were already jumping into the first stage of my crisis without even being asked. All I had to do was start things going with the Tekeli waking up, biting off a sailor's leg and then massacring most of the NPCs, including Captain Nakhona.

I moved seamlessly into the escape crisis. I decided to give Zoja and Safi bonuses for some of the rolls because they had torches. In the next chapter, fire is an important weapon and here's a hint of things to come. When the Tekeli-spawn swarm the lighthouse, they will know that fire's their best weapon.

But no one asked to stand and fight when the Tekeli woke up and began eating their companions. Jack asked if he could send his bird, Popoki, to help his uncle when they were running away and Hoka got impaled by a strand of Tekeli-goo.

That wasn't in my game notes, but that's okay. Hoka doesn't *have* to be dead and if Jack's role-playing some familial devotion, then I'm going to do my best to play along. But when I asked if he wanted Popoki to attack the tentacle or try to grab Hoka, Jack hesitated and decided not to risk his pet bird. Which is good, because I probably would have killed Popoki. (After which I would have refunded Jack the points that went into his bird. I'm not a *total* asshole.)

So Uncle Hoka died, Kaikoa took some sanity damage watching him get torn to pieces like a dog with a squirrel, and everyone ran for the temple doors.

There was a massive sanity damage hit in this crisis. Seeing the semi-liquid monster coating the temple surge to life and slaughter people with limbs and mouths that rise out of the goop is pretty horrifying. Gavril and Zoja were already down to single-digit sanity, though. There was no way – even on a successful roll – for them to resist all of it. Or even enough to remain sane.

It didn't seem fair to hit them with sanity damage that they had no hope of resisting right in the first ten minutes of a session, so I lowered it. Which still left a lot of sanity damage. Gavril and Zoja still didn't do very well, but they were able to spend every bonus they had to scrape through with a single point of sanity left apiece.

Did Zoja and Gavril earn any derangements? No, they got off a little easy and with no permanent scars... yet. But Cedar and Bryan also had to use up a lot of resources to achieve that small victory, so they earned their success and felt like they had to work for it.

Players panting on the couch after a narrow escape is good. It means they're excited. I don't have to screw their characters over to accomplish that, which is much less fun for them.

When everyone escaped the temple, Jack asked if the doors had handles and could be closed behind them. Nope, no handles. But I asked if he had any ideas for pulling them shut. Everyone else just kept running – including Alak'ai and Danya – so Jack understandably didn't want Kaikoa to stick it out alone.

I gave the players a brief moment of hope when the Tekeli hesitated in the sun, but then it recovered and surged out of the temple.

Everyone ran like hell to get away. When the characters got back to the *Iron Eel*, they were all shouting just as loud as Alak'ai to get the ship into the water. Everyone – even Safi – grabbed a rope to drag it back into the ocean and they all jumped on the oars to help make their escape.

I didn't make very much of a crisis out of sailing away, though. I had beaten the characters all to hell. At this point, throwing another handful of rolls at them or carving off a few more points of health wouldn't have accomplished anything, so I dropped it and let them run for their lives.

And that's the end of Chapter 1!

I handed out chapter rewards and was completely unsurprised when all four players chose a sanity bonus from the list of perks I offered. But wrapping up the first chapter took less than an hour and everyone was all warmed up, so I opened my Chapter 2 notes, reviewed the first scene, and then kept going.

CHAPTER 2

The Hunter

So the first scene of Chapter 2 is pretty much a description of the trip back to the lighthouse, and the action doesn't really start until they reach The Hunter. But my players like to role-play, and they certainly had a lot to talk about. I described the day's frantic rowing and then had Alak'ai replace the characters with fresh workers so they could rest, which gave them time to talk.

Danya crouched in the bow of the ship and Alak went to talk to her, leaving an opening for anyone else to join him. Erica said she was all over that, but had something quick to do first.

Which turned out to be sucking up to the two mercenaries. Safi thanked Zoja and Gavril, then gave them each one of her doses of alcohol. Booze gives bonuses for resisting sanity loss (and penalties if you drink more than one dose), and it's in Safi's self interest for the best-armed, highest-damage characters in the group to be, you know, sane. The last thing Erica wants is for Gavril to mistake Safi for an evil anemone and stab her in the face. And she wants them invested in keeping Safi alive.

As I've mentioned, Erica loves to draw other players into scenes. So Safi asked if Zoja and Gavril were siblings, married, or partners. Which got curt answers from Zoja of *no*, *no*, and *yes*. It was nice and in character, but it didn't make for much of a scene, so Safi asked how they started working together. Zoja told Gavril to tell the story.

Hehe, Bryan didn't get to sit quietly the whole time. Fortunately, he and Cedar have talked about how their characters are connected and he had a story ready to go. Gavril said he had been hired to kill the man that Zoja was hired to protect. He said she fought well, but they came to an arrangement – Gavril paid Zoja the same wage she was getting as bodyguard to just stand aside.

Safi asked in horror if Zoja accepted and the mercenary replied only that "salt is good." Salt is the base of currency in Korvath, so that's true enough. Safi asked if Zoja got paid by her client up front, taking his money and then Gavril's, too, and Zoja just repeated that salt is good. Knowing that they intend to be vague and change the story with each telling, I wonder what their story will be next time. Maybe they flipped a coin? I don't know, but I look forward to it.

Confused and alarmed, Safi excused herself and went to check on Danya. No one else followed, so it was just Erica with Alak and Danya for this scene. Danya thanked them for helping her, but Safi admitted that she was dragged out to the temple and didn't deserve thanks. Erica doesn't want Safi to be entirely despicable, just selfish. She's an ordinary girl, not a criminal mastermind, and she only wants to live through all this. But she's from Miskaton and she's a scholar – Erica's curiosity always comes through in her characters – so Safi asked Danya what happened in the temple.

Danya doesn't remember much, so there wasn't a lot for me to do except to try making her a little pathetic. The same for when Safi asked about the Tekeli. Alak'ai excused Danya from rowing and walked aft with Safi.

Since the players seemed to miss Danya's use of *a* Tekeli instead of *the* Tekeli, Alak said it was that comment that worried him the most. And after I had him point it out, I managed to get the shudder from the players that I hoped for.

Safi asked to borrow Alak'ai's spyglass – with a wistful comment about her father's stolen telescope – and looked back. She couldn't see the island anymore, but *did* see the Tekeli. Alak explained that on the open sea (to the best of my Googling), the horizon was three miles out and the *Iron Eel* had traveled more than thirty.

Which meant either the Tekeli had spread from the island all the way here, or else it was following them. Alak wasn't sure which one was more frightening.

Only Safi participated in that conversation, but all the players reacted with shouts and shudders, which is the kind of shit I love as a Storyteller.

Alak'ai asked Safi to draw up the map of the island she offered before things got spooky. After some stammering – that had been a bit of a lie; Safi's educated but no cartographer – she asked him why. They escaped the island. Alak asked if she thought the temple wasn't dangerous anymore. Safi shook her head and agreed to make the map as best she could.

Which got Safi into Alak'ai's cabin and some alone time with ink and paper. She also took advantage of this opportunity to riffle through his room, though Safi got distracted by Alak'ai's star charts and thoughts of home, so she didn't steal anything.

When Safi was done with the map – which Erica made a mental stat + art roll for and did pretty well – she curled up on Alak'ai's bed and cried herself to sleep after their narrow escape. Erica's familiar with the Mythos theme and is gleefully traumatizing her character.

No one else had anything to do during that first day of escape except for Kaikoa playing with the icky healing shell I created. Jack seemed pretty excited about it, so yay.

I narrated the night's rest and calculated healing, though everyone was still a little bruised, mentally and physically. The characters woke up and found the Tekeli still behind them. They had to take their shift rowing and Bryan sang, "Row, row, row the boat very effin' fast!"

Good to know that I'm keeping them on edge.

While Danya and Safi rowed, they talked. Danya was excused from work, but she was determined to do her part. (I really need the players to like Danya and not ditch her again if she is going to serve her story role. I could use the metaphorical stick and *force* the party to keep Danya close with orders from Alak'ai, but I'd rather use the carrot and make them *want* to have her around.)

Safi warned Danya to keep quiet about the Tekeli and what had happened in the temple. Alak'ai seemed nice – he didn't kick Safi out of his room even after discovering her takeover of his bed – but the Kels don't trust sea-eyes and it wouldn't take much after their misadventure for Danya to get herself thrown overboard.

During a break in the rowing, Safi asked the other lighthouse prisoners if any of them were trained healers, trying to find some help for Danya. Most of the criminals weren't caught trying to steal back their father's telescope. They were sentenced out to the coast for killing people and being generally more awful, so the answer was *no*. But Safi had the idea that mercenaries might know how to stitch themselves up – because Erica is great at finding reasons to involve other players in scenes.

As it turns out, Gavril did have some medicinal skill, although it was mostly for the purpose of creating poisons... Which he made certain to mention. But Safi asked if he could check Danya over for head wounds, hoping that was the extent of her strangeness.

Gavril answered that he knew about poisons, not broken girls, which riled Safi up. She defended Danya heatedly, but Zoja said, "If the ground shakes and a jar falls off a shelf, is not the jar's fault. But jar is still broken."

Gavril finally relented, though. He checked Danya and found no wounds. Danya asked the two mercenaries if they would protect her from the Kelanua if they got angry with her. Zoja has sea-eyes too, right? Zoja agreed that they both had blue eyes... but that was it. Wow, Cedar's playing it pretty cold. In fact, she had Zoja tell Gavril a minute later that next time they're getting paid up front, or they're taking their salt and leaving.

Now, Cedar and Bryan have been gaming with me for almost two decades and I'm not too worried that they're going to *actually* turn tail and run. They'll find a reason to stay and help The Hunter, if only for the promise of more salt along with some nice hazard pay. They're just role-playing a new fear of the sea.

Speaking of healing, Safi asked if the ship had a healer. She was still injured and Safi was probing to see if they would help Danya instead of drowning her. I had the *Iron Eel's* healer talk to her in broken Antoran, trying to convince Safi to use the dreamcap – the luminescent jellyfish with the psychotropic sting. Safi freaked out at the "tentacle-fish" and ran screaming out of the healer's cabin. Erica really knows how to play up the horror.

Jack had no intention of missing out on that shit, so he decided that Kaikoa was on his way to see the healer, too. He seems to like to have Kaikoa nearby, listening to other peoples' conversations, but not really participating. Remember that Kaikoa knows the Antoran language, but almost never speaks it. When he asked the healer in Kelanua what that Massir girl's problem was, I dropped the broken speech and got to show that it was mostly an issue of language barrier. Which I suppose wouldn't have been a problem if Safi had busted out her Kelanua, but she's trying to keep her knowledge of her jailer's language on the down-low, too. It helps her take advantage of situations for her own benefit.

Being Kelanua himself, Kaikoa had no problem with the dreamcap sting, of course. And when I gave Jack the sanity healing and bonuses, Cedar and Bryan suddenly got real excited about getting stung.

Jack described Kaikoa being comedically high because of the dreamcap sting and Cedar used that as a lead-in to getting some sanity healing herself. She asked Alak'ai why the scout was acting so strangely and he mentioned dreamcap. Alak speaks Antoran and doesn't conceal that fact, so he was able to send Gavril and Zoja to the healer with a clear understanding of what was on offer.

Both happily took the sting and the sanity healing, and Bryan got excited about the toxin. Didn't I predict that he would come up with a project and try to invent a new poison or something?

Gavril started trying to talk to the Kelanua healer, attempting to convince her to extract some of the venom for him. Bryan intended to use it for sanity protection more than on Gavril's knives, which is a good idea. They can't carry around jellyfish in their pockets, but a vial of toxin is pretty portable. I had some fun purposefully misunderstanding, and the healer said *no*. But I don't give it long before Gavril sneaks in to play with jellyfish – with or without permission.

Erica wasn't out of things to do on the journey back to the lighthouse, though. Safi was a prisoner and never got to sleep in a bed or even in private, but she doubted that Alak would give her his room again – not unless she was asking to share it with him, at least. But Alak'ai had excused Danya from rowing because of her ordeal on the island, and Safi wondered if she could leverage the other girl's mental condition for a private room.

So Safi suggested to Alak that Danya would benefit from some peace and quiet, then offered to keep an eye on her. Alak'ai let them have the captain's cabin, since Nakhona died on the island and left it empty. The girls got a bed, and Safi got to rummage through the dead captain's stuff, scoring some booze to replace what she gave Zoja and Gavril. Safi also got Danya's backstory about trying to be a mercenary in Athol, then killing one of the boys who tried to rape her and being sentenced to The Hunter.

I concluded the session when the characters finally spotted The Hunter jutting up from the horizon. The Tekeli still chased them, spreading from north to south. (The horizon was only three miles, but still – a three-mile-wide living evil oil slick!) I hit them with a bit more sanity damage and the mercenaries failed hard again, but the healing kept them from going insane just yet.

We hardly got into my Chapter 2 notes. The players had tons of their own scenes to play out and were happy to do so. There was only one crisis and no combat, but it was exciting and everyone had a good time. I hope they enjoyed the relative quiet because the rest of Chapter 2 is pretty much non-stop crises and combats.

The Siege

Session 3.

But before the non-stop combats and crises, the characters all had to report back to the lighthouse keepers at The Hunter. Their conversation was largely with the Keeper of the Tower, commander of the lighthouse, but I mentioned the Kelanua advisors under her: the Keeper of the Ships, the Keeper of the Lamp, and the Keeper of Salt. But none of them really matter much to the story, so I kept focus tight on the Towerkeeper. Who I gender-swapped at the last minute.

I didn't want to make my players have to recount the game so far, so I described Alak'ai giving a summary. But then Keeper Lukoa asked the other survivors what they saw, offering them a chance to give their input.

Zoja mentioned that fire was the most effective weapon against the creature, so I had the Towerkeeper talk about their stores of fire weapons here instead of when it was outlined later. It also gave me the opportunity to point out that at low tide, the stores are also low. Why stockpile weapons to defend the land from the horrors of the sea when the sea is at its least frightening?

Lukoa told the two mercenary characters that they earned their pay and they deserved a bonus, and the Saltkeeper would arrange payment. Then Lukoa said it seemed there was another fight ahead and asked if they would stay.

And here's where I waited to see what Cedar and Bryan would do. Gavril said that they should take their salt and leave, but Zoja asked where they would go. She pointed out that if the Tekeli got onto dry land and came after the Antoran city-states, there would be no place to spend their earnings.

Cedar confided that she's been thinking Zoja has another side. She aspires to be... well, not exactly heroic, but let's say *epic*. More than anything else, Zoja wants to be renowned and remembered.

Cedar has been internally developing this aspect of Zoja that drives her to stick out the most terrible situations.

And Gavril agreed without question because he's her partner.

I wasn't sure how they planned to stay with the story, but I knew they would find a way. Now it's my turn to make Cedar and Bryan glad they did, while making Zoja and Gavril regret it.

The next order of business lay with the Shipkeeper. Nakhona was dead and now the *Iron Eel* needed a new captain, so Alak'ai got a promotion. I'll need him to be in a position of authority to help me steer things back on course if they wander too far afield, but I had Alak offer the now-vacant first mate's position to Kaikoa, which wasn't in the original notes. He told the scout to think on it because I didn't want Jack to feel pressured. He likes playing the scout, the spy, the guy who runs out into danger – often without warning anybody else first. I wasn't sure if he wanted a position of responsibility or how he would handle it.

Lukoa ended the meeting, but I wanted to give the player characters a chance to take care of any business they might have before plunging into the siege.

Safi engaged Alak'ai right after the meeting, pursuing her character goal of doing as little work as possible and staying out of any danger. Safi argued that with the Tekeli on its way, it didn't seem like a good idea to send the prisoners to the mine. Alak'ai said they were being used to position the lighthouse's siege weapons, but that didn't strike Safi as any safer a job. So she persuaded Alak to send her and Danya to clean out Nakhona's cabin, then to move his own stuff in. Danya said she wanted to fight, but Safi stood on her foot and got them the softer job.

Alak'ai told Kaikoa to take Safi and Danya down to the *Iron Eel*, and Jack decided to stop off at the lighthouse's apothecary to see his grandfather. I expected Jack to show his grandpa – the lighthouse apothecary, Kaikiki – the weird-ass healing mollusk that he found. But instead, Kaikoa told Kaikiki the news that his son – Uncle Hoka

– had died in the island temple. Kudos to Jack for going after the emotional scene.

They mourned together for a bit and *then* Jack whipped out the healing shell. I didn't really have anything else to tell Kaikoa about it, but had Kaikiki ask him to leave it overnight to study.

I cut back to Zoja and Gavril to give Bryan or Cedar a chance for any scenes they wanted to run, and to take care of business. They didn't have anything to role-play at the moment, but they did take their salt pay and loaded up on healing items, as well as lots and lots of alcohol to help resist the sanity damage. I might get to smack them with some drunkenness penalties, or maybe make alcoholics out of them.

Down on the *Iron Eel*, Erica had a stack of conversations queued up. Jack wanted Kaikoa to wait outside the captain's cabin because he likes to eavesdrop. If anyone wants to have a talk that he doesn't know about, they have to *really* work at it. But first, Safi just begged Danya to stop asking to fight because she wasn't going to survive.

Danya wanted to be a mercenary, and I had to stay true to her background. But Safi said that if Danya kept volunteering for trouble, she couldn't protect her. It was sweet and given Danya's background, I figure that she didn't have a lot of loving support. So if Safi didn't already have Danya's devotion, she certainly had it now. And because Safi is willing to do just about anything to stay safe, she advised Danya to cry if she had to. Safi's already pegged Alak'ai for a soft touch, so Erica plans to have her character hide behind him in battle, and hide behind his authority when it comes to work.

And loot his ship, apparently. Safi searched the cabin and I had her find some jewelry belonging to the late Captain Nakhona. I had given Bryan and Cedar some cash for their pay, and Kaikoa had the option for a promotion, but Safi was a prisoner. She didn't get paid, so I figured I could let her loot a bit. But I did let her know that the Kelanua weren't going to trade supplies for stolen Kelanua jewelry. She would have to fence it first.

But remember how Jack likes to listen in on conversations? He asked if Kaikoa could hear when Safi and Danya were trying to pick the lock on the captain's chest. He did well, and Erica failed her roll. When Jack wanted Kaikoa to sneak into the cabin quietly and catch them picking the lock, though, this time *he* messed up and Safi got to close the chest without getting caught.

Erica had opted not to re-lock it, though, which Kaikoa quickly discovered when he tested the lock. Normally, our group doesn't do a lot of inter-PC conflict. My players would rather be fighting monsters or whatever than each other, but Jack hasn't gamed with us as much and I didn't know how far he was going to take it.

He found a knife Danya had managed to take and confiscated it, but then said she could have it back when she was done working for the day. So really not that bad, as far as PC conflicts go. I've been with groups where that scene would have come to blows.

There was only a little bit of back-talk, and Kaikoa responded to Safi and Danya's Antoran speech, which revealed that he knew the language. Safi fired back that she understood Kelanua, too. But in the end, both agreed not to tell anybody else about the other one's linguistic facility.

The worst that came out of it was that Erica couldn't have Safi break into Alak'ai's things when they went to pack up his room, and that Kaikoa threatened Safi with something gross under her pillow.

I checked in with Bryan and Cedar again to see if they had anything else for Gavril and Zoja. Cedar *did* have something this time. When the Towerkeeper announced turning on the warning light and the bells sounded, Cedar thought it would be a good idea for Zoja to know what the hell all of those bells meant.

Zoja went searching for Alak'ai to ask him about the bells, if there were different bells for different attacks, and what the emergency procedures were. The Kelanua are a close-knit community, so they rely more on experience and custom than procedure. But Alak explained the bells they might hear during an attack, and he gave some respect to the pair of inlander mercenaries who bothered to learn some Kelanua ways.

We did the evening's recovery, healing and such. Everyone was pretty much healed up now, but sanity is a little harder to recover. Safi fenced her jewelry for a few spare coins and smuggled salt in the prison barracks, then I went into the next in-game day.

In the morning, Kaikoa told Alak'ai that he wanted to accept the offer to be his first mate. I think Jack kind of liked bossing Safi and Danya around. So they went up the lighthouse to tell the Keeper of Ships and make it official, and stopped off at the apothecary to pick up the healing shell from Kaikiki. I just had the old apothecary tell Kaikoa to keep it wet so the mollusk doesn't die. When the group goes inland and loses ready access to seawater, I might have Jack make some nature skill rolls to keep his psychotropic healing shell-fish alive.

Zoja wanted to see if the Tekeli was any closer to shore today, so she and Gavril went up to a balcony. Cedar was very specific that she intended to look out in the daytime, without any telescopes or other optical enhancement. She didn't want to risk sanity losses for getting too good a look at the Tekeli.

Which was just sitting on the surface of the sea, being evil soup. It bobbed over the waves and the dark edges undulated, but it had stopped advancing – which earned me a resounding *uh-oh* from the group. Players know that when the evil thing isn't doing something obvious, it's going to do something worse.

Other than the conversation with Keeper Lukoa, all of the other scenes were made up on the spot and/or player-generated.

But then The Hunter's bells rang out for the first Dekara attack. I got to put the warning into specific terms for Cedar and Bryan because their characters had learned about the bell codes, and they rushed right to the location of the fight. Alak'ai and Kaikoa were on their way up the tower, so when the bells rang, they rushed outside to the nearest balcony, which was the one Zoja and Gavril were at.

Alak'ai had collected Safi and Danya to have them move Kaikoa's stuff into the first mate's cabin, so I got them there, too, and it was all nicely plausible.

This fight was against the crab-monsters again, so the players all knew what to expect this time. And since this was the third fight of the campaign, they knew their characters' abilities a little bit better, too. I was still able to hit them with some sanity damage, though. So there.

My players had a good feel for their attacks and used them well, including trying a combo mechanic we're testing out. Some of their attacks have the combo attribute. When they hit, they put a stack of combo on the enemy that carries one of their abilities. When they hit an enemy target with a stack of combo on it, they can put another stack on, or they can trigger the existing one. So if Kaikoa puts his bleeding combo on a giant crab, then Gavril hits it and triggers the stack, he gets to add bleeding to his attack.

I wanted some rule mechanic to leverage teamwork and I hope that the combo attribute will let each character put their attacks' flavor out there for some big combined hits. We're trying combos out for the first time in Tydalus, so we'll see how it goes. Maybe it'll need a second draft, or maybe it will just suck and we'll never use it again.

The Dekara in this fight were the same basic-level monsters as the first combat, so they can only survive a few hits, but when I start busting out the bigger monsters – like the Tekeli spawn – I think combos will get some real play.

The truth of adult role-playing is that most of us have work in the morning and can't game until IHOP is the only restaurant still open, so we ended this session after the fight.

The rest of Chapter 2 is still a lot of combat and crises, but with one fight down already, it may not be as crowded next week. And if it goes too quickly and doesn't feel *enough* like a siege, then I can always add another combat or a second wave to one of the fights.

Perhaps I'll resurrect the siege weapon crisis that I discarded between the second and third outlines.

I'll see how things are going next session and what feels right.

Session 4.

Before we started up game, I asked if anyone had experience to spend. (We're using an expenditure-based system, not a level-based one.) My players asked if they could buy some kind of skill or ability to help with the sanity loss on alertness checks. Something to let their characters peek through their fingers and see just enough not to be surprised, but maybe not see enough to piss themselves.

That sounded like a pretty good idea, and I quickly invented an attribute that I called *Willful Ignorance*. No one had enough experience to buy it right now, so I haven't had to nail down specifics yet. I'm thinking that it will be a small penalty on alertness checks, but some permanent damage reduction on sanity damage.

It's nice to know that my players are already terrified and asking for ways to blind their characters to the horrors of Tydalus.

We started game this session on the blood-stained balcony from last week. More warning bells rang in the lighthouse and the group was off to the next scene, fighting the Dekara while dangling from ropes off the side of The Hunter.

With Safi being a coward, Erica gave the whole crisis a big *nope*. She knew that she was willingly stepping out of a scene, and that she might not have anything to do during that time. But I already had the mini-crisis for Danya sleep-walking off the balcony. It was supposed to come after the attack, but Safi has already bonded with Danya. So I used it to both give Erica something fun to do and add chaos to the situation.

Safi had to tackle Danya to stop her walking right off the ledge. I also substituted a few rolls for her to help the others in their crisis checks by managing their ropes, even as she tried to talk Danya literally off the ledge.

Gavril ended up being the one with a Dekara hanging off of his foot at the end and there were so many failed rolls that he almost lost a foot. But Zoja came in at the last minute and saved his ass. Well, his foot.

Signs & Portents

I sent the PCs directly to the next Dekara battle inside the lighthouse to keep the pressure on. They charged into the combat with half their health and energy gone, so they fought conservatively – for the most part. They made good use of slowing attacks to keep the Dekara at bay, then Zoja ran in because her axe skills give her bonus damage the more she's surrounded. You would think I'd be able to put the hurt on her, but Zoja's a Cuisinart of death.

The Dekara hard-shells – larger versions of the standard crab-monsters with some more health and armor – gave the group some good play with the combo mechanic. They lasted long enough to stack up some levels of combo and trigger the big hits.

It was the first time that the combos really got any play, so we'll have to see them in action a few more times before I know how well they work.

Erica also asked if she could use some of the vodka Safi bought for resisting sanity loss to make Molotov cocktails. I didn't give her much in the way of complicated rolls since it's just stuffing a rag into a booze bottle and lighting it, but she made some checks to toss Kaikoa a bottle – almost lighting him on fire – then I had to invent the damage for it. I decided that the bottle breaks and splashes in an area, inflicting ongoing burning damage.

The players did an excellent job and their characters came out bloodied but victorious. Next I get to whip out the Tekeli spawn, though.

Danya babbled all through the rope-battle crisis, so her little info dump had already happened instead of occurring here. But she mentioned the Sign in the next scene, so the title for this section ended up being rather inaccurate. I'm the only one who sees my silly scene names, though, so who cares?

Tekeli-li

Beat up and drained from a crisis and then a fight, the characters pressed on. There was some lead-up in this scene, with the Tekeli dividing into the horde of oozing spawn that made everyone but Jack shiver. Apparently, I'll have to really up my creepy game to get a reaction out of him.

But the horrible sight of the Tekeli spawning came with sanity damage and it hit them hard. Even Kaikoa and Safi lost some sanity. Despite trying to numb it all with booze, Gavril and Zoja took the full hit.

And that did it for their sanity pools! Cedar and Bryan grinned and said they would start thinking up what kind of derangement their characters will get. But for the time being, we went on with the game. Best to give them the week between sessions to come up with something both fun and horrible than to bring game to a stop to hash it out.

Besides, I had a Tekeli spawn to throw at them.

The characters all bravely rode the ropes down after Alak'ai – well, Safi screamed the entire way – into the bowels of The Hunter and the scene where I set the battle with the Tekeli spawn. And the picture I chose for the spawn's token didn't endear it any more to my PCs. It was *full* of teeth and eyes and more teeth.

The player characters didn't exactly charge in to attack. Back on the island, they saw swords and harpoons splash harmlessly right through the Tekeli. Gavril and Zoja fell back on their bows, figuring they could afford to lose some arrows, while Alak shouted for fire.

All the fire weapons had been moved to deal with the Tekeli, and now a spawn was inside the lighthouse. Actually, I decided to have it seep into the salt mines, near the prisoner barracks.

The bows were secondary weapons for the mercenaries and did very little damage to the Tekeli spawn, but Safi grabbed a lamp and spent her actions soaking strips of cloth from her shirt in oil so they could make fire arrows.

The Tekeli sludged forward slowly, but it's an amorphous blob and its tentacles gave it range enough to smack Zoja. Hard. So far, Zoja's never been hit like that, so it made an impression.

Next round, Erica used Safi's actions to set up Gavril and Zoja's quiver so they could shoot flaming arrows, which at least did full damage to the Tekeli. But it got to do some damage, too. Zoja took the brunt of it like a good tank, but after the other fights, she wasn't in shape to tank much longer. I came to the rescue with some NPC's dragging a barrel of pitch into the mines at the end of the round.

So the first thing everyone did the following round was to soak their melee weapons in pitch and light them up. More confident now, they waded in for the up-close kill. With their primary attacks finally doing full damage, they cut quickly into the Tekeli spawn's health, but the monster also got to dish out its close-range splash damage, almost driving Zoja to zero health and injuring Kaikoa's bird. And killing several of the NPCs who had brought the barrel before they could fall back.

Jack called Popoki away. He wasn't about to risk losing his bird just to get its NPC bonus each round. Still, the characters managed to beat the Tekeli spawn down to zero health and it retreated. Yep, not died... just squelched away and poured itself back down the cliffs, into the ocean. (Gavril and Zoja stayed behind to bind their wounds, so only Safi and Kaikoa followed Alak'ai to make sure the spawn was leaving.)

White Sails

It wasn't lost on my players that the evil ooze was only retreating, not dying. And they weren't happy to see the Tekeli reabsorb its singed spawn, but then reinforcements from the other lighthouses arrived to drive the parent creature back.

I closed out the session with Danya mumbling that the Tekeli fears only "the Sign," setting up the next chapter.

It was a pretty action-packed session this week. Half of the characters came damn close to going down and taking a scar. Gavril was one failed roll away from losing a foot and Zoja was a round from dropping, too. And even though they didn't take a scar, they get to pick derangements! My fond hope as Storyteller is that no one will end this little game entirely sane.

Chapter 3 has a long sequel section, where the characters get to catch their breath, discuss Danya's strange intuitive knowledge and how they can get this Sign she spoke of. They'll get to recover most of their health and sanity – I'm betting that they'll be begging for a dreamcap sting – just in time to send them out and lose it all again.

All in all, a successful session.

CHAPTER 3

Wild Gull Chase

Session 5.

I had some work to do between game sessions. I reviewed my notes about how derangements worked – including phobias, nightmares, and addiction – because Cedar and Bryan had to choose one for their characters. I also took another look at Willful Ignorance, the new attribute that will basically be the power to witness horrors from beyond human understanding, close your eyes and stick your fingers in your ears to block out the screams.

When we sat down for game this week, Cedar already knew the derangement she wanted for Zoja. Alcoholism, of course. I gave her the rules and she said, "Wow, that sucks."

In short, whenever Zoja takes a drink, she has to make a roll or else consume an extra dose of alcohol, drinking through her supply faster and subjecting her to the penalties that come from getting increasingly drunk. But then Cedar smiled and said, "Well, derangements are supposed to suck. I like it."

My group occasionally plays short, one-night RPGs. Sometimes it's to fill in gaps between major campaigns, sometimes it's just to get a taste of something different. We often set these one-nighters in the Lovecraft Mythos, and everyone knows the story will be difficult and horrible, and that their characters will die or go mad. The characters collect scars, curses and derangements until they either die or become unplayable, then the player makes a fresh character to feed into the meat-grinder of the Mythos universe.

So all of my players for Tydalus – except Jack, who's never done a one-nighter with us – are used to loss of life, limb and mind in our games. They even take a perverse, cathartic pleasure in it. They will argue about whose character did the most awful thing, who died in the most horrible fashion, or be proud of being the first to get eaten by a monster. It's really different from our usual games. But they know Tydalus is a horror story, and they've bought into it. We'll see if Jack gets into the madness.

Speaking of madness, Bryan needed some help picking out a derangement for Gavril. Fortunately, I already had one in mind – PTSD. It's terror-agnostic, so it works for any horrible thing, and just gives Gavril a penalty on resisting sanity loss. That sounds bad – and it is – but Gavril's mental stats are not his strongest area. His chances of succeeding in any sanity defense are already so low that a penalty doesn't really make much difference. But it also incentivizes him to hit the booze harder to cancel out the penalty, and Gavril will have to drink more to get a bonus.

Then everyone got excited when I laid out the finalized rules for Willful Ignorance: a one-point bonus to resist sanity damage, and all sanity damage is reduced by five. That means all the little creepy things, the small hits, are probably reduced to zero even on a failed defense, which is pretty powerful.

Jack expressed interest in buying Willful Ignorance, but I had to point out that Kaikoa isn't willfully ignorant. In fact, our scout *likes* poking his nose into the shadows, looking under the rocks, going out alone to investigate the weird noises in his underwear, and the other horror movie tropes that get you killed. We'll see if Jack starts steering Kaikoa in a more cautious direction, or if he'll stick with the macabre thing that he's got going now. And I'm not sure yet if anyone else will buy the attribute, or if they would rather just take the sanity damage. We'll see.

Once Cedar and Bryan had their derangements picked out, and everyone spent what experience they had saved up, we got started with their characters watching the Tekeli retreat before the flaming bombardment from the Kelanua reinforcements.

Alak'ai said he had to go report to the lighthouse keepers. They needed to know that the Tekeli might have a weakness – "the Sign" that Danya muttered about all through the attack. But Safi followed Alak'ai, worried that Danya's insane (but informative) rantings were going to get her thrown off the top of The Hunter. Safi even asked how much it would cost for Alak to not mention the Sign, or at least not mention Danya. Alak'ai asked her why, and Safi admitted her fears. He reassured her that they need Danya and won't kill her. Safi wasn't convinced, but she's a prisoner of the lighthouse and doesn't get to give orders.

Erica's totally bought into protecting Danya and is looking out for her with all Safi's weaselly powers. It will be great when Danya turns on her in the final chapter.

Meanwhile, Gavril and Zoja returned to the mercenary barracks to clean their wounds, get drunk and fall asleep. Other than some semi in-character jokes and jabs about Gavril bandaging the wrong foot when Bryan screwed up a medicine check, they didn't have any scenes to play out.

So that left Kaikoa with Danya, who had been left behind by the others. Kaikoa went to the apothecary and for lack of orders, Danya followed him. Jack just wanted Kaikoa to get more healing supplies, but after the battle, the corridor outside the apothecary was packed with the wounded and dying. To his credit, Kaikoa offered to pitch in. He's Kaikiki's grandson and the best healer in the group.

Jack asked if he could make Danya his assistant, so I gave him a leadership roll to see if she would be underfoot, just stay out of the way, or actually be helpful. Jack succeeded his roll, so Danya gave him a bonus on his medicine check to help out with the wounded. I told Jack that if he rolled well enough, Kaikoa could earn a level of influence with The Hunter as he saved lives. Jack succeeded in the check, but not well enough for the influence. Maybe next time.

Safi didn't get to follow Alak into his meeting with the keepers, so she returned to where she had left the others. But everyone else had wandered off to pursue their own stuff. What's a prisoner to do when left unattended in a lighthouse?

Steal stuff, apparently.

Safi decided to take advantage of the Kelanua being away or – let's be honest here – being dead. Erica did fine on her rolls to sneak around their homes and storerooms without being caught, and well enough on her rolls to break in. But Erica said that she wanted to prioritize cash/salt and medicine, so I gave her a roll to make sure she stole high-value items – which she failed. I narrated Safi finding clay jars with what looked like salves and unguents. She grabbed them and then went looking for her prison buddy, Danya.

I made Safi ask around and gave Erica a streetwise roll to find where in the massive lighthouse Danya was (with a small language barrier penalty because she still didn't want to reveal her fluency in Kelanua), and she finally discovered Kaikoa was letting Danya stay in his family apartments.

That was some more off-the-cuff world-building. Where do the Kelanua live in their lighthouses, anyway? I figured they lived in extended family groups in large suites. A big common room, with smaller bedrooms for the various families.

But because the Kelanua population is on the decline, there are all too many empty rooms and Jack agreed that after the death of Uncle Hoka, his family was down to just him and Grandpa Kaikiki. Kaikoa let Danya have an empty room instead of sending her back to the prison barracks. When Safi showed up, he extended the offer to her, as well.

Once she was alone with Danya, Safi shared her ill-gotten haul. Since Danya spent the afternoon working as an impromptu nurse, she helped Safi look at the medicine jars. But the Kelanua didn't develop much of a written language and don't label anything. (The great scholar Alhazred used Massir letters to write Kelanua songs, giving them a written language which most Kels still don't learn.) With Danya's help, Safi found out it wasn't salves she had stolen – it was someone's makeup.

Safi complained bitterly about the Kelanua's lack of writing, but then she decided that nothing would drive away the horror of the battles they just survived better than a makeover. So she and Danya made each other up. Does makeup defeat the horror of the Tekeli? Not really, but spending some time with a friend and finding something to laugh about after a week of nothing but horror and bloodshed? That's worth some sanity recovery. And it was sweet to watch Safi tell Danya she was pretty.

The next day, the party gathered and Alak'ai told them that The Hunters' keepers wanted to speak to them. On the way, they passed the apothecary and discovered a commotion over a man who had broken in during the night and stuck his entire arm into the dreamcap barrel, overdosing on jellyfish stings.

The sight of the man stung/drugged until his consciousness was stretched to breaking caused some sanity damage, but there wasn't anything that the PCs could do for the guy and they proceeded to the meeting a little shaken.

I figured that the meeting would go as laid out in my notes, and for the most part, it did. The players received the quest to sail north to The Nautilus and research the Sign. But when the Towerkeeper asked Danya what the Sign was and how she learned about it, Safi answered to Danya's name. Erica knew that they met the keepers before, but the prisoners hadn't been introduced to the lighthouse leaders. And Safi didn't want Danya's blue sea-eyes giving them any excuse to drown her, so she pretended to be the other girl. The rest of the characters kept their mouths shut and backed Safi up.

Safi handled the questions well, but there wasn't much to ask or tell yet – which was why they're being sent to The Nautilus, anyway. But Safi did get excited when the Towerkeeper offered freedom as a reward to the two prisoners if they banished or defeated the Tekeli.

Getting away from the ocean and going back home to Miskaton is all Safi wants.

Kaikoa volunteered to go – he lives in The Hunter and is Alak's first mate, after all – and both mercenaries also agreed to take the job. Lukoa gave the characters until dawn the following day to gear up and ready the ship.

Unsurprisingly, Gavril and Zoja loaded up on alcohol, buying as much as they could afford. Jack doesn't seem to think he needs to worry about Kaikoa's sanity, so he got some healing supplies. Safi – the best negotiator of the group, obviously – did some epic haggling and bought plenty of booze *and* healing supplies, most of which she plans to give out to the others to make sure they like her enough to keep protecting her.

They also returned to Kaikiki to take care of their wounds and sanity. That meant dreamcap stings. Erica stuck to her guns there, playing up Safi being phobic of anything from the sea – which will probably be an actual derangement before this game is done – but Gavril asked for two stings. That recovered most of his sanity, but if having excess alcohol gets you drunk, then excess psychedelic jelly-fish venom makes you trip balls. Bryan really hoped there wouldn't be another attack and that Gavril would get to sleep off his dream-cap hangover.

Since Safi didn't get anywhere near the dreamcap, she hit the bottle that night and got drunk with Danya. And Erica decided that two drunk girls trying to cope with trauma might seek comfort with each other. Safi and Danya have been getting close, protecting each other, and it might turn into a romance. And here I thought Alak'ai would be the obvious romantic interest for Safi.

Again, finding human connection when surrounded by death is worth a little sanity. I wouldn't have given Safi any sanity if she was doing it just to get it back, but she was starting the ball rolling on a romantic arc, and that's well worth some reward.

Setting Sail

Kaikoa woke Safi and Danya up in the morning, and Jack – who is a meddler and likes to mess with the other players a bit – decided to sneak in and go through Safi's pockets while she slept to make sure she hadn't robbed his uncle's room. He *did* have a point – Safi steals pretty much everything that isn't nailed down.

Jack rolled a stealth check, Erica rolled alertness, and Safi woke up shouting as a strange man snuck into the bedroom. Which woke Danya up. And she's a rape survivor, so she pulled her knife. When Kaikoa tried to touch her and comfort the girl, she flinched. Danya said, "They don't knock in the prison, either. I'm used to it."

Jack felt bad when he realized that Danya had some trauma and that began a change in attitude toward her. We'll see how far it goes.

But onward with the campaign! Since the next scene was sailing away from The Hunter and around the Tekeli with only a barrier of dwindling fire to shield them, I played it for tension and gave everyone an easy sanity check. Cedar remembered Zoja's alcoholism and she was already drinking. She failed her addiction roll and made that two drinks, so her sanity defense was actually pretty good. And then Cedar rolled a critical success to resist the sanity loss.

Because she got a critical success, I gave Cedar the opportunity to buy off her addiction defect at reduced cost. But Cedar actually hesitated.

"I just got this derangement and I haven't played around with it much," she said.

I love that my players are so eager to role-play their characters, including their faults and flaws. But ultimately, Cedar decided to buy the defect off while she could, since she was sure her derangement would be back soon.

When the *Iron Eel* finally made it out past the Tekeli, Safi and Danya lingered at the aft of the ship, watching to see if it would follow. Benefits of being key players on this quest: they didn't have to row with the rest of the prisoners anymore. The Tekeli stretched out some pseudopods after the ship, but didn't give chase.

There was some early suspicion in the group that the Tekeli was only following Danya. Bryan and Cedar actually contemplated discretely offing her a few times.

Well, that was a good idea, so I decided to have some of the Kelanua sailors accuse Danya of bringing the Tekeli down on them and being generally bad luck. There has been a lot of worry that Danya's sea-eyes will put her in danger – and Cedar took sea-eyes as a flaw for Zoja – so I wanted that danger to manifest.

Safi argued with the sailors, actually placing her cowardly self between Danya and the angry sailors. But Safi's arguments were a little heated and amounted to "stop being superstitious and stupid ass clowns." That went over about as well as you would expect it to, so Safi shouted for Zoja.

Jack wanted Kaikoa to overhear, of course, so I gave him, Zoja, and Gavril some initiative rolls to see who jumped into the argument first. Jack won and stepped in. Which is what I was hoping for, actually – I had Alak'ai make Kaikoa first mate and I wanted him to actually have to do some leadership stuff.

But what do players do when the NPCs insult or threaten them? They insult and threaten right back, of course. It's a rare player who doesn't. So Kaikoa leapt with both feet right onto the *you're all ignorant dumbasses* wagon. Even when the other sailors got to speak in Kelanua and no longer had to make their points in broken Antoran, Kaikoa still wouldn't back down.

When Zoja and Gavril got involved, the angry sailors just included the Strazni mercenary in their *throw the sea-eyes overboard* pitch. Kaikoa actually translated the Kelanua into Antoran so Zoja and Gavril could hear all of the arguments and insults. That only made Zoja aggressive, and didn't calm the situation down one bit.

The sailors reluctantly downgraded their plan from chucking Danya and Zoja both overboard to just putting them ashore at the next lighthouse, but Kaikoa still toed the party line – like any loyal player character would. Zoja had her hand on her axes and was inviting the Kelanua to try their luck, but all of the bickering had bought Erica some time to think. She jumped back in with some Safi-style begging and wheedling. Talking her way out of things is what Safi was built to do.

Safi smoothly assured everyone that they were all on the same side, fighting the Tekeli together. The monster was the enemy and Danya was their best chance at stopping it from destroying their home. The sailors agreed and eventually left Danya alone, but they weren't very happy about any of this.

I planned on having Alak'ai talk to Kaikoa about the incident once he heard about it from the sailors, but Jack decided to tell the captain himself. Alak'ai agreed Kaikoa was right about Danya, but pointed out that the first mate of the *Iron Eel* just took the side of a bunch of foreigners against his own crew.

Jack's jaw dropped. He hadn't considered that angle at all. He had played the scene like most players would, working with and for the party, and being a bit of a smartass about it. Jack forgot he was a leader now, basically. It's understandable – he did what players do, and the sailors were being superstitious and bigoted, so they were in the wrong. But Alak told him that the crew has to follow Kaikoa's orders, and they need to be able to trust him. They won't be on his side if they don't think he's on theirs.

Alak'ai said Kaikoa didn't have to apologize – again, the sailors *were* in the wrong here – but Kaikoa did need to repair their trust. Jack took it well, and he has to look at his character in a new light. Now he knows that he can't be snarky to everyone. Not that Kaikoa won't be snarky to other people off the *Iron Eel*, I'm sure, but it was a good encounter.

After that, Erica figured Safi and Danya should probably lie low for a while. Alak'ai had said they could sleep in the crew quarters instead of with the other prisoners, but with at least a percentage of the Kelanua crew sharing the opinion that Danya will bring evil down on them – though it was clear the Tekeli wasn't following her – that didn't seem like much of an upgrade.

So Safi asked Kaikoa what it would cost to let them use the first mate's cabin to hide out. Kaikoa needed something to help smooth things over with the crew, so he offered his cabin for a considerable portion of Safi's alcohol.

Deal. Safi and Danya got their private room – more for survival purposes than amorous ones. But before taking his new booze to share around, Kaikoa found Gavril and asked him to please teach Danya how to use her little knife before someone got killed. I had planned to have Danya ask the two mercenaries to teach her how to fight – that's been her life-long dream, after all – but it's better that the players are taking steps and getting their characters involved.

Kaikoa's next destination was the crew bunks. He had to sleep there since he was renting out his cabin to the girls, and he wanted to talk to the three sailors that he confronted. Kaikoa poured them all drinks and apologized. He said that Danya was the only one with knowledge about the Tekeli and they need her alive to stop it. The sailors grudgingly admitted that was true, but said that they didn't need Zoja.

Jack had to think fast, and Kaikoa countered that they *did* need Zoja and her axes because she's a badass. Jack laid it on a bit thick, talking up how Zoja chopped the Dekara to pieces like kindling, but he also gave them the hope that the big mercenary's sea-eyes are her *own* bad luck. Maybe evil will be attracted to Zoja and away from the crew. Like a shit magnet. The monsters will go for Zoja first and she'll either kill them, or else the monsters will take care of their Zoja problem.

Win-win. That was something they could all drink to.

The trip up to The Nautilus took eight days, but that's a lot of sequel time. Time enough for everyone to do pretty much everything that they need to and play out all their scenes, so once we settled on what everyone would generally spend their days doing, we fast-forwarded a bit.

...To the scene where the *Iron Eel* is attacked by a monster. Since my monster is a sort of angler fish-like sea serpent, it had a glowing light that was *very* creepy. So I gave everyone a dice roll to notice a glow following the ship.

And I ended the session there. Combat takes the longest to play out and it was getting late. All the pizza was gone, so we'll start next game with the sea monster attack. This session was all role-playing and it was a good one. I think after the non-stop combat and crises of the lighthouse siege, my players needed the rest and sequel time. They're getting more into character and developing attachments to each other.

Erica, Bryan, and Cedar are all nervous about getting attached. Characters in cosmic horror stories rarely get a happy ending. The overriding theme of the genre is inhuman, inescapable doom and they're dealing with forces that can't be killed – that which is dead cannot die, you know – and any victory is temporary at best.

But they're having a good time and in a perverse, twisted sort of way, they're even looking forward to their hideous fates.

Session 6.

At one point, I actually thought that with only four chapters, we might finish the whole game in a month. But *nooo...* My players like to role-play and shit.

My revised estimate? Ten weeks. Maybe a little bit more if Erica really works her romantic arc.

Before starting game this weekend, everyone who had experience spent it. Cedar got the second level of Zoja's military training, making her a bit tankier. Jack raised Kaikoa's medicine skill. Bryan purchased an ability for Gavril that would improve his initiative, and Erica got... I forget. Some skills, probably. Safi is the skill-horse of the group.

Since I ended the last session with an eerie light following the ship, we began with rolling initiative!

My angler-fish-dragon thing had some big bite-based attacks, but I also gave it a lure attack that inflicts sanity damage, defended with mental stats instead of physical, and then compels the target to move closer. My players did *not* like that one, even though I didn't manage to get any of them to walk into the sea serpent's mouth.

Actually, I didn't get to land all that much damage on the party. Zoja did her job tanking *far* too adeptly. She took all of the hits and took them well. But everyone remained on their toes and played around with their combos. In just one round, they had five levels of combo stacked up on the monster and then triggered them all in a massive hit. A single enemy with lots of health makes for a different dynamic and combo strategy, so everyone had fun with it.

Mid-combat, I had the dreamcap barrel spill over. Everyone had to roll not to get stung by hallucinogenic jellyfish. Even though no one failed, they all reacted with fear. The suicide by jellyfish they had witnessed at The Hunter was pretty horrific.

But remember how Bryan loves projects? And how he liked the dreamcap? In the middle of the battle, he spared some actions to scoop up a jellyfish in one of his poison jars. I gave him a roll for it and was kind of hoping he would do poorly enough to get stung, but no. Well, it would have given him sanity back anyway and then how would I drive the PCs out of their minds?

Actually... Jack had a big monster with a magic light on its head and he *wanted* that light. Kaikoa collects monster parts, so he took the penalties to aim for the angler fish light and cut it off. I decided to have some fun with Kaikoa's macabre collection, but it did take away my monster's glowing lure attack. Jack saved Zoja and Gavril from some sanity damage, but I figured that Kaikoa would take it all later.

When they beat the fish-dragon all to hell, I had it retreat. As monsters go, this is just some kind of freak eel and doesn't rank up there with the truly terrifying shit in the depths of the Ryllic Ocean. So, not a lot of animals are going to fight to the death, and having it stick around wouldn't prolong the fight much anyhow.

They still had a few day's travel up to The Nautilus and my next scene, so I asked if anyone had anything to do during the trip. And oh yes, did they ever. So that fight was the only part of my notes we got through this week.

Kaikoa had his shiny new trophy, which he stashed below decks until they were sure the angler thing wasn't going to come back. But as soon as he had a chance, Kaikoa went back to examine the light. The fascinating, wonderful light...

Kaikoa took some sanity damage and when he wanted to dissect the lure to find out what made it glow, I had Jack roll to even bring himself to harm his precious light. And he failed. When Kaikoa left to go back up into the fresh air, he had to roll to leave the lure, but that time he succeeded.

Safi had a request, so when Kaikoa emerged, she asked him if she and Danya could hide out below decks. Erica is keeping Safi's distrust of the ocean on high, which is nice because it promotes the level of anxiety a good horror game should have. Kaikoa agreed – easy, since the girls had been using his cabin anyway – and invited them both to look at his special light. Safi didn't think that keeping a bloody chunk of monster was as cool as Kaikoa did, and decided against borrowing the first mate's cabin again.

Gavril and Zoja washed off the monster blood, and then they talked. Zoja asked how Gavril's head was doing, if all the trauma was getting to him. She had spotted her partner grabbing the little dreamcap and wondered if he was hard up for some relief. Gavril insisted that he was fine, which Zoja said was a damned good thing. After all, the songs of their glorious battles would suck if the last verse was about how Gavril went nuts and stabbed Zoja in the back.

A legacy of mountains of dead enemies and fame is emerging as Zoja's core motivation. She doesn't want to die before becoming the most renowned warrior on Tydalus, and wanted her name to be as famous as Rhystar and Zelleny's. Which was Cedar's way of leading into something else...

Zoja had a revelation. Zelleny was a Strazni prophetess and she foretold the disaster that sunk Antora. And Danya has been given insight into the Tekeli and Dekara, just like Zelleny. Zoja decided that Danya's not crazy or broken – she's *holy*.

First of all, huge props to Cedar for weaving the world lore into her character and running with it. Secondly, Zoja has joined Safi and Kaikoa in taking Danya under her wing. And her protection – Zoja told Danya that she would guard her and even train her. This will work perfectly with rescuing Danya in Dunspire and then her betrayal in Chapter 4. I can't wait!

Zoja figuratively offered Danya her axe – not literally; she loves those axes – and started training the girl. And with Danya's backstory, it was pretty much a dream come true. Gavril remained more skeptical about the religious aspect of all this and didn't exactly buy into the idea of Saint Danya, but he always follows Zoja's lead.

Danya asked how a Falspire assassin and a Vanhome mercenary ended up becoming partners. Cedar and Bryan got to cackle and play with their backstory. This time, Zoja told the tale and said that when Gavril came after the person she was protecting, they fought. He was the best she'd ever been up against. She knocked Gavril on the head at last, but when he woke up, Zoja put in her two-week notice and set off with him to become the greatest mercenary duo in Korvath.

Safi was right there with Danya and Erica had already asked for their *how did you meet* story, so she noticed the different version. But Safi just scratched her head – Erica didn't want to ruin Bryan and Cedar's never-tell-the-same-story-twice thing. Some players would call them out on it, but from a narrative and/or comedic standpoint, it's better to let them tell half a dozen stories first, then call them out on it at the end of the game.

And the truth will probably be that Zoja and Gavril both just got drunk, then woke up with a hangover and a partner.

Jack wasn't interested in religious revelations or mercenaries, so he had Kaikoa go back below decks to take another look at his light. And it was fading... When you cut the angler lure thing off a big sea monster, it's not going to glow forever. I was hoping to get Kaikoa into a frenzy of trying to keep it glowing. I didn't really think that I would get him as far as sacrificing crew members to make the light happy, but I was hoping he would try something.

Jack *really* wanted to cut it open, though. I'm not sure what he expected Kaikoa to find, but he finally succeeded in the roll to risk harming his precious light, so he sliced it up. And let out all the glowing goo, which promptly lost its light. Kaikoa took some more sanity damage, but that was it for my light and Jack got to dissect it like he wanted.

Erica wasn't done, either. That night in the crew bunk – because even though Safi is a little survivor and didn't want to push her luck with superstitious sailors, she absolutely refused to sleep in a cabin full of monster guts – she talked with Danya about being called a prophet and getting trained. Danya said that she loved learning to fight, of course... but also that she felt like she needs to dig into her strange knowledge so that she doesn't disappoint Zoja. And Danya asked if Safi thought she was a saint, too.

Safi's a scholar from Miskaton, so she's skeptical and trusts only what she can see or measure. But Safi's seen some strange shit, too, and a prophetess wouldn't be much weirder than intelligent crabs. Danya said that she was going to pray, which let me bring up that element of Tydalus a little more, and send Danya slowly off toward the deep end.

Safi left Danya to it, and went back up onto the *Iron Eel's* deck. They had stopped for the night at The Dolphin, another Kelanua lighthouse on the way north to The Nautilus, so with shore leave for the crew, I was able to give everyone lots of space.

Safi ran into Kaikoa on deck, taking his bucket of monster bits to dump because the light was gone. Safi kept clear of that process, but they spoke a little and Safi said something about going home, which Jack took to mean that she intended to run away.

Hmm... Erica *has* said that at some point, Safi's going to make a run for home, but she hasn't really been doing anything suspicious. It seemed to me like a little out-of-game knowledge on Jack's part, and he went so far as to set his bird to spy on Safi.

But players do things like that, so Erica just shrugged and went with it. We're pretty sure that Jack will come down on any attempt to have Safi run away and cut it short, but Erica can just plan with that in mind. She's not actually going to have Safi leave the story, but her options for how and why she brings Safi back might end up a little limited.

There was still some time left, though, so I dangled Alak'ai out on deck. Maybe not literally, but I had him using that spyglass of his, which is pretty much guaranteed Safi-bait. Erica bit, of course, and Safi came over to find that Alak'ai enjoys stargazing. Not just to navigate the sea, but because his grandfather taught him the stars and constellations.

I hit Safi right in the daddy issues. Not that I planned it when I gave Alak'ai his hobby back in the early outlines, but when Erica came up with her father's stolen telescope as the crime that had her sent to the lighthouse, I knew exactly how to use it.

Safi and Alak compared constellations, trading the Kelanua and Antoran names. Was Safi flirting with Alak'ai? I wasn't quite sure – she was sleeping with Danya, but she certainly seemed to be taking an interest in Alak, too. I made a mental note, but Erica wasn't done with the scene.

Safi asked Alak'ai why he spoke such good Antoran and I answered that his grandmother was from Dyrah. She was one of the merchants who brought supplies from the city to the lighthouse, where she met his grandfather and eventually decided to stay. Safi noted that he was nicer to the prisoners than most and Alak said his grandmother taught him to speak Antoran, but also taught him that inlanders weren't *all* uncivilized. Safi was a bit scandalized, but if she decides to romance Alak'ai instead of Danya, then we laid out some good groundwork.

And all that was out of my ass. In my notes, I had worked out the stargazing bit, but I hadn't exactly drawn Alak'ai's family tree. It explained Alak a little, though, and Erica liked it. So it worked.

After Safi asked if Alak was familiar with Zelletar, the Antoran religion – which he was – Safi also shared Zoja's revelation about Danya. Alak agreed that he should really know if Zoja was going to defend Danya with religious fervor, especially when half of his crew wouldn't mind drowning both of the sea-eyed women.

But Safi had an ulterior motive – she asked Alak'ai if he would take care of Danya, too. Because out-of-game knowledge or no, Jack was right that Safi plans to make a run for it, but she also wanted to be sure that Danya would be safe.

We called game there after an evening of good role-playing. All of my players had scenes that they wanted to run and had some excellent interactions. We added to the world-building, too. And we only got through a single combat scene from my notes. I may need to revise my estimate on this game's run-time again.

The Nautilus

Session 7.

I spent the week considering NPCs – specifically Alak'ai. Does the story still call for him, or should I remove the guy?

One fewer NPC for me to run is always nice. I can get carried away with creating NPCs and in one past game, I had something like seven of them who were regular companions for a while before

I was able to whittle that number down. It was pretty epic when all of the PCs' friends came back for the final battle, but it was also exhausting for me to manage.

Cutting Alak'ai from the game would mean I only need to play Danya on a regular basis. Alak'ai is also around so that if none of the players are willing to sacrifice their character at the end, I have someone to feed to the Elder Sign. But Erica would probably enjoy a dramatic flip and giving Safi a moment of heroic bravery after a game of cowardice. I also have Zoja, who is quite literally religiously devoted to Danya, and who wants to be famous. Sacrificing herself to save the world will pretty much guarantee her a song or two.

So I don't need Alak'ai around for the final sacrifice. Do I need him at all? Safi's in a relationship with Danya, but she's also taken a clear interest in Alak'ai, too. I'm not sure if she will switch gears, but I don't like to curtail my players' options.

The other thing for me to consider is Alak's role in directing the plot. Not to force my players to stay on the rails, but to guide them back to the plot in case they get lost. Alak'ai has earned the characters' trust and if he makes some suggestion, I can reasonably expect them to follow it. (But as always, part of building that trust is not giving the PCs guidance when they don't need it.)

If I remove Alak'ai – probably by killing him, and probably in some kind of gruesome, sanity-damaging manner – then that leaves Kaikoa in the highest position of power. But by now you have seen what kind of player Jack is. He's as capable of dramatic scenes and deep character interaction as anyone, but he is a shit-stirrer. Jack might be able to lead the group, but he'd lead them into trouble just for the hell of it.

If I thought that Jack had his eye on being captain or wanted to try his hand leading the party, I would give him the metaphorical crown. But I think he took the offer of first mate for the same reason that he's obsessed with collecting bits of monster – just for the hell of it. I almost feel like it would be punishing Jack to give Kaikoa all that responsibility. And he doesn't have a strong sense of the story. We're not close enough to the finish line that I feel safe removing too much guidance.

So I've decided to keep Alak'ai around for the time being. If I change my mind, I can always kill him horribly later. But I'll just keep Alak's touch as captain light and see if Kaikoa wants to lead. Jack *did* reevaluate what it is to be first mate after his screw-up. And when they finish at The Nautilus, the characters will be heading inland, where Alak is going to be way out of his element and taking a back seat anyway.

Alak'ai might be sticking around for now, but the first thing that happened when we sat down to game this week was Safi making a run for it. The ship was still docked at The Dolphin, so she snuck away from Danya – leaving most of her gear behind for the Strazni girl – but when Safi got up on deck and had to creep away, Erica rolled a critical failure. I had Safi knock over a rack of harpoons that went clattering across the deck and everyone else got a check to wake up. Both Kaikoa and Gavril sprang out of bed, but Zoja slept through it.

Safi had to choose between trying to pretend that she had just come to investigate the noise, or bolting. And Safi booked it. It turns out that Safi's good at more than talking her way out of things – she's also really good at running away. She had a head start against Kaikoa and Gavril, and though her stealth rolls may have sucked, there was nothing wrong with her dice when it came to hauling ass.

When Gavril and Kaikoa lost track of Safi, they returned to the ship to report to Alak'ai. He advised not climbing around the cliffs in the darkness and said they could send scouts out in the morning to follow the roads, search the lighthouse, and check the shore for Safi's body if she fell. Jack and Bryan left it at that, I think because they know Erica wouldn't actually abandon the story.

But Kaikoa did have to break the news to Danya that Safi had left her. Poor Danya.

Safi didn't remain gone, though. She hid out near The Dolphin for a little while, but then broke down and slunk back to the *Iron Eel*, where she was met on deck by Alak'ai. Since I knew Erica intended for Safi to stay, I got to play the nice guy again. Alak'ai gave Safi one more chance to run, promising that he wouldn't report it until she was long gone.

But Safi said that she was staying. When asked why she ran, Safi answered that it was because she was afraid. But then why did she come back? Safi told Alak'ai that she couldn't leave Danya. So Alak asked if she loved Danya, and Safi said she didn't know.

Kaikoa and Gavril accepted Safi's return easily enough, though they told her not to try that little stunt again. Danya was both hurt and pissed, so Safi gave her some space. But I think my favorite line to come from Safi's escape was when Gavril explained to Zoja what happened and she said, "Safi came back? She might be the craziest one of us all."

With that done, the rest of the trip to The Nautilus was largely abstracted. Gavril and Zoja trained Danya, and Kaikoa decided to show her how the Kelanua fight. Everyone wants to make the crazy girl into a badass. Safi stayed away from Danya, so she spent time with Alak'ai and there was some more confused flirting.

I think Erica's laying groundwork for a romantic arc with him, too. She might go with Danya or Alak'ai. Or perhaps both... I don't know. But Erica has options and since no one else is doing any kind of love story, all the romantic interests are hers to play with.

The *Iron Eel* arrived up at The Nautilus, where the meeting with Keeper Mairanda and her ancient uncle Mel'ai went as outlined in my notes. The characters listened to their fragment of song – which I didn't even attempt to sing – and then got to search through the Kelanua library. That sparked some fun conversation, since The Nautilus is the only Kelanua library. Alak'ai and Kaikoa were awed by the sight, but Safi had almost as many books just in her house back home in Miskaton. And Zoja can't read at all.

So needless to say, Zoja didn't help with any of the research rolls and Bryan opted to have Gavril nap in the corner or dice with his partner while Kaikoa and Safi worked. Danya just looked over their shoulders.

But Safi's a little scholar and we can add research to lying and running away on her list of skills. Erica almost aced the research successes on her own. Kaikoa's contribution put her *way* over.

While they were working, Kaikoa found the Azif – Alhazred's final book and the one that drove him into madness – and flipped through it for some sanity damage. Safi, being the scholar that she is, simply couldn't resist reading it. I had to jack up the damage for doing more than skimming and Safi lost more sanity from reading that book than from all the monsters and weird shit so far.

But in the Azif, Safi read Alhazred's translations of Cthyan and she spent some experience to add those languages to her list. I had Danya correct her pronunciation, which freaked out both Safi and Kaikoa. (Finally, I creeped Jack out!) I also pulled some stuff on the origin of shoggoths out of my ass so that I could give Safi a little info on the Tekeli. Nothing actually helpful for fighting it, but including a reference to the Sign which binds the polyps that fly beneath the ground and repels the horrors that fly beyond the stars.

While Safi and Danya were reading from the Azif, Kaikoa found Gavril and Zoja nearby. He confronted Gavril about the dreamcap that he stole during the sea serpent attack, but it was more curiosity than confrontation. Gavril tried to play ignorant, but then admitted that he took the dreamcap because he was interested in its venom. Kaikoa offered to teach Gavril how to care for them, since a jellyfish won't live very long in a tiny jar, and they decided to work together to extract the venom.

Jack and Bryan made some skill rolls and came up with enough of the dreamcap toxin to overdose on. Kaikoa took a little to the girls, where Safi said that Danya needed it more. Since she was answering questions in Cthyan – which she claimed not to know –

Kaikoa agreed. And it occurred to everyone that putting Danya into a dreamcap trance might unlock more of her strange knowledge.

Safi actually went down to The Nautilus' apothecary and broke her firm no-tentacles rule to get stung by the jellyfish. Reading the Azif really compromised her sanity, but she wanted to keep sane for Danya. I was *so* close to bringing Safi down to derangement levels. But she recovered some. A lot, actually – Safi took two stings and was high as a kite.

When Kaikoa and Danya caught up to Safi, she thought Danya was a hallucination. That was Erica's input, not my narration. Safi said that she wished the real Danya would talk to her again, playing with the hurt feelings her escape attempt had caused.

The party slept in empty quarters up in The Nautilus that night and Danya forgave Safi. She told Safi to hold her and promise never to leave again. Which Safi did, so they kissed and made up. Aww...

Inland

But the characters found the full song and now it was time for the inland stuff. The lyrics talked about a place under the aurora, but where the people didn't lose their minds. Somewhere in that was the location of the Sign. Or so my players hope.

So their characters set out the next morning to search the cities and villages in the northern mountains. They were already talking about using Danya's strange knowledge to home in on the Sign. They're putting more trust in Danya, and using her creepy insight more and more, which is perfect.

I used Alak'ai to remind the group that The Hunter was under siege by the Tekeli and that they had to move fast. Then he asked how exactly they could move fast without a ship and Zoja said that on land, the answer was horses.

The Bhataari of Antora were a nomadic people, and the Strazni and Massir both rode, so they brought horses when Antora sank.

Horses were one of the advantages that allowed them to conquer Korvath in the first place.

But mountains aren't the best place to raise horses, especially when half the dry land tends to flood and you have people to feed. So horses on Tydalus are very expensive, and the characters already blew all their money on supplies. Mostly to buy alcohol.

I think the best part, though, was when Zoja mentioned horses and Kaikoa stared blankly, asking what the hell a horse was. Jack grew up with horses and raises them. In fact, he had come to game right after a show, where he and his horse took four second-place ribbons. A horse show in the morning, then pretending he doesn't know what horses are in the afternoon. It was amazing.

Horses weren't even a possibility until they reached a city. So the characters set out on foot and walked a few days to Ashmont, one of the two large northern Antoran cities and the nearest major peak to The Nautilus. Nothing much happened during the trip, so I skipped up to the city itself, where the Kelanua characters were awed by all the trees and gardens. Ashmont's entire economy was based on its forested valleys and slopes, and for men who split their time between a lighthouse and the ocean, it was all new and astonishing.

Jack followed Alak'ai's lead on the surprise. If you want to give your players a little input on how to react without just telling them, model that reaction with an NPC. Jack saw Alak being surprised by all of the trees, so he had Kaikoa react the same way.

You know the investigation will lead them up to Vanhome. But my players don't, and the map places Ashmont just as northerly, so the party very reasonably wanted to investigate the area and I had to handle that. Here goes some unplanned investigation!

In Ashmont, the party split up. Safi took Kaikoa and Alak'ai to ask around for local legends of hallowed places, hoping to find the Sign. Gavril and Zoja took Danya to find fighting work and earn a few pounds. (Since Korvath is on the salt standard, their money is the *pound*, with each coin being worth one pound of salt.)

I handled Safi's task first. After all, if she found the Sign in Ashmont, they didn't need to travel any further.

Safi took the two Kelanua men and began her search at the local church. I silently blessed Erica for that choice. Thanks to her, I got to describe a proper Zelletaran church so that the players will be able to see the differences between this one in Ashmont and the blasphemous cult cell later on in Dunspire.

At the Ashmont church, the priestess was friendly with Safi, but suspicious of Kaikoa and Alak'ai. She invoked the blessing of the Star of Zelleny, which is supposedly the star that Zelleny navigated by to lead the refugees to Korvath. It's the symbol that Zelletarans trace on their chest for good luck, like making the sign of the cross. I've even got Erica tracing the sign in character while we sit there gaming, and I bet that I can get Cedar doing it for Zoja.

And yeah, the star bears a deliberate resemblance to the Elder Sign that the characters are searching for.

But the priestess could tell Safi of no specific hallowed locations in Ashmont. Erica asked about old places, hoping to find some area the Cthyans shunned when this was *their* city, but was built over by the Kelanua and then built over again by the Antorans... So that's a tough thing to research.

Alak'ai suggested asking the city's elders, who surely knew the songs of this place. While Antorans don't really keep an oral history, people *do* like telling stories, so Safi searched a park replete with people to talk to. She got an afternoon's worth of reminiscing and folktales, but nothing that pinpointed any hallowed ground.

Safi might go search city records. If there's a part of Ashmont or a village that was built after the Cthyans – something first built by the Kelanua or Antorans – then it might be a place they avoided. But the day was running out both in and out of game.

I switched back to the deadly duo – Gavril and Zoja, with Danya along as their trainee mercenary – and gave them a streetwise skill check to find some paid work, but then I called game for the day.

We were nearing the end of the session and I wanted to take the week to come up with a fun job for my hired swords.

That was it for the game session, but after everyone else left to head home, Erica and I talked about mercenary jobs. First, we had to figure out some more details about Ashmont. I hadn't expected the characters to spend so much time there and now we had to do some emergency world-building before I could figure out what sort of jobs might be available.

That stuff about Ashmont being the primary lumber producer was the only specific world-building we had done for the city. We did have a line about how the people who live there take the long view of things, since their business is raising trees. Seeds planted now take decades to grow into trees large enough to harvest, and the people of Ashmont are the same with their plans. That's pretty good, but we needed to know more.

I'll spare you all of the false starts and ideas that didn't gel, and skip to what we finally landed on.

The king of Ashmont owns all the Kingswood, the large forest covering the peak of Ashmont. The smaller mountains and valleys of the range are each owned by a noble family, collectively referred to as the Grove Lords. The Grove Lords of Ashmont each maintain a royal copse, which pays a tithe of wood to the king. They keep the rest of the forest for themselves.

The Grove Lords and the king each have a force of well-armed rangers that patrol and protect their forests, and fosters who plant, care for, and then harvest the trees.

So the simple job we came up with was this: one of the Grove Lords bribed the chief ranger of a rival lord to poison some of their trees. Maybe even the royal copse, which would offend the king and would certainly mean that the wronged lord would have to pay the tithe from their own trees. The chief ranger has the loyalty of the rest of the rangers, though, so the Grove Lord can't even punish his own corrupted agent.

This Grove Lord wants to hire someone to get rid of his chief ranger, but then make it look like the work of the rival lord. That removes a disloyal agent while keeping the loyalty of the rest of the rangers, and simultaneously gets them pissed off at the rival. That will make it less likely for the next chief ranger to accept a bribe, and open the door for a retaliatory strike in the future.

It's not the most complex task, but I have a day job to work and I only have a week to put this all together for game. Plus, Erica and I realized that the party is heading to Vanhome eventually, and when they get there, we want a better picture of that city, too.

So we had more world-building to work on. But we're doing it ahead of time, so it's not an emergency. Vanhome was the first city that the Antorans conquered when they arrived in Korvath, being the closest to the land bridge. The refugees had lost Zelleny and Rhystar to the tidal wave, so they had no leaders. And there was a war against the Kelanua to fight, so leadership fell to war chiefs and generals.

To this day, Vanhome selects their leadership from among their best warriors. Whenever a king or queen of Vanhome dies, there is a tournament – only open to citizens of Vanhome and its villages – and whoever wins is crowned the new monarch.

Of course, the royal and noble families of Vanhome are able to afford the most skilled fighting tutors and have the best chance at the crown, so most monarchs come from among those rich families. But that's not to say that there haven't been a number of gifted peasants who fought their way through the tournament and ended up ruling Vanhome.

The need for training means that fighting schools sprang up all across Vanhome. When one of their students fights their way to the throne, the school that taught them gains the status of *crown school*. (Or three-crown school if they've trained three kings or queens, etc.) Crown schools usually enjoy the patronage and thus wealth of the ruler that they trained. The smaller schools keep their doors open on the hopes – and payment – of peasants and merchants' children who dream of fighting in the next tournament.

There are always mercenaries and soldiers to teach, as well, and Antorans from other cities who want to learn the best martial arts. So there's plenty of business, even when a young monarch is ruling Vanhome and there's no tournament on the horizon.

The competition leads to rivalries and the schools often get into duels – tentatively referred to as *pride matches* – to prove themselves, avenge insults, protect reputation, or even to take out students who look a bit too promising when the royal tournament is looming.

Anyway, lots of potential stories and history here and we sent the results of our brainstorm to Cedar so she can have all this info for Zoja. I expect that she'll blend it into her backstory, and since she's already given Zoja a desire for fame and glory, I think it'll be a good fit.

I feel a bit more prepared to present the cities of Ashmont and Vanhome next week. I'll come up with some ranger stats so Bryan and Cedar can beat some down, name some Grove Lords, and then I'm ready to go.

Session 8.

Alright, I whipped up a scene for my mercenary PCs. I have a contact for the job – a lesser ranger for Lord Olros who is named Khalil. Olros has a rival, named Lady Erdene. And I have Olros' traitorous chief ranger, Helma. I'll send Gavril and Zoja to one of Ashmont's towns, Firth, where Olros rules, to confront Helma at the tavern, the Old Stump.

I had fun making the chief ranger a dual axe-wielding woman to match Zoja blade for blade. I'm not sure if Cedar and Bryan will want to gather the whole group or leave them to their research in Ashmont, but I know that they'll be taking Danya along.

Normally, Danya only grants an NPC bonus against monsters because her strange insight doesn't reveal the weaknesses of normal humans. But three out of four of the player characters have been teaching Danya various forms of combat. And the only reason Safi hasn't made a contribution on that front is because she's a bit of a wet sack herself.

So I'm upgrading Danya's NPC bonus to one that works against human opponents, as well.

While we're on the subject of my players' investment in Danya, let's examine that. Safi is in a romantic relationship with her, Kaikoa has taken her under his wing, Zoja is nearly fanatically devoted to her and Gavril... Well, at least he'll do whatever Zoja does. Danya has turned out to be the one that brings them all together, which is a hell of a change from Chapter 1 when they very nearly let her die. Twice – first during the tentacle attack, then again in the temple.

So what changed? Well, this kind of thing just sort of happens over time when the players interact with an NPC. The more they interact, the closer they grow. Just like real friendships. Assuming the NPC or friend in question isn't an asshole. And Danya's nice. Troubled, but nice.

But let's compare her to Alak'ai. So far, Safi is the only one who talks to him much. The mercenaries have received a few orders, but neither one has ever had a scene alone with Alak'ai. Kaikoa's had more conversations with his boss, and that wonderful scene where he got a rough lesson in leadership. But Jack's been more focused on Danya and experimenting with monsters. He could have latched onto Alak as a mentor figure, but just didn't take it that direction.

Don't get me wrong, I'm not complaining. Everyone is following the story. Extra NPC interactions are just that – extra. But it seems worth talking about how it shapes the non-player characters. I do this all the time without thinking about it, but writing up this guide and doing a post-mortem on every game session helped me understand what's going on, so you get to see me learn a lesson here.

I give my NPCs quirks and goals – like Danya's mercenary ambitions and Alak's love of the stars – but that's only half the equation. The players actually pick and choose how an NPC develops based on how they interact.

Jack didn't make a mentor of Alak'ai, so his leadership experience has taken a back seat. But Safi is interested in why Alak'ai is nice to her and Danya, and so his kindness gets the spotlight. Alak is a gentler figure in the story because that part of him has received attention. Danya was going to be a pitiable character, but everyone's working overtime to teach her strength, so she is becoming scrappy instead.

Pay attention not only to which NPCs your players seek out to interact with, but which aspects of their personalities you should develop. If you ignore what your players like about an NPC, they will probably lose interest in interacting. That doesn't mean that you should toss the NPC's goals and motives out the window, but let it shape and alter *how* that NPC goes about them.

Okay, that's an interesting insight into my own Storytelling, but now it's game time. The characters have a corrupt ranger to murder and horses to buy.

...Cedar and Bryan got sick, so there's no game this week.

Damn.

Everyone is finally feeling better! But it's now been nearly two weeks between games and we all might be a little rusty. So I'll start with a little recap of what everyone is up to in Ashmont, then give the players a bit of time to reacquaint themselves and get back into character.

I placed Zoja and Gavril in a tavern, then had Danya ask how they got into mercenary work. The prompt served both to give the players some dialogue to help them get into character, and also to let Cedar talk about any new details of her backstory taken from the information we gave her about Vanhome. Though apparently Cedar read my email, but didn't decide on anything. Oh, well.

We know that Zoja is illiterate, so I figured she didn't come from a noble family and probably didn't go to a crown school. Cedar said she always imagined that Zoja's mother was a mercenary. I asked if her mother had carried Zoja around while fighting, or if she was retired. I suggested that Zoja's mom had opened a school of her own, teaching out of a hovel to peasant hopefuls with dreams of at least training a future monarch, and her own dream of becoming a crown school. So Zoja learned from her mother.

Instant backstory... Which Cedar reduced to a one-word answer for Danya. Bryan was equally terse in relating Gavril's backstory to their new student.

But their incredible lack of detail and narrative sense was about perfect for getting them in character, so then we launched into the job that they rolled to find last time instead. Zoja and Gavril were pointed to a man very conspicuously trying to look inconspicuous at the end of the bar.

"Noble house?" Gavril asked.

"Rich idiot," Zoja agreed.

I had fun with it and Danya asked what to do now. Do they go over to the man? Do they invite him over? Gavril walked up and provoked the man a little, telling him he was failing to blend in. But then Gavril invited him over. And so they met Khalil – Lord Olros' ranger, and one of Helma's less loyal subordinates. Khalil wasn't a rich idiot, but he works for one.

Cedar and Bryan got the story on Lord Olros, Lady Erdene, and the traitorous ranger, Helma. Neither Gavril or Zoja have very good mental stats or political skills, and they did terribly on their roll to parse the political nuances of Ashmont. So they decided "Screw it, let's just kill her." They'll have to wing some way of making the hit look like it was ordered by Lady Erdene.

Last week, Erica had concerns about giving the players a hit job. My gaming group likes to play the heroes. I've played with some who prefer to be anti-heroes, lean toward the dark side, or are just plain rogues. But my current players are more of the rogue-with-a-heart-of-gold type, when they're not just rolling straight-up heroes. We've all played everything at one point or another over the last twenty years together, though. Even sweet Cedar, who usually plays our healers, once rolled up a spine-removing demoness. And just look at Zoja.

But Erica wanted me to have a backup plan in case they weren't willing to kill someone, even if I made the target a traitor. Needless to say, I had a nice little I-told-you-so moment as Bryan and Cedar discussed the best way to whack a corrupt ranger. They didn't even consider sparing Helma's life.

So Gavril, Zoja, and Danya left Ashmont to hunt down Helma. Which left Safi, Kaikoa, and Alak'ai in the city... with no money. They couldn't afford an inn room and the woods were patrolled by rangers who protected the trees. I gave Erica and Jack a roll to hide their camp, and Safi and Kaikoa wisely agreed to avoid lighting up a campfire.

That meant Safi, Kaikoa, and Alak'ai would all have to huddle together for warmth. Erica considered briefly, then had Safi decline because cuddling with Alak was too tempting. Safi ran away from Danya once and she never wanted to hurt her again, regardless of any confused feelings for Alak'ai.

Safi's got herself well-positioned for a love triangle and she did it well. And she told Alak'ai that he was too tempting, so now he knows that he's one of the corners. I didn't have him push things at all, though... I'm trying to play Alak as a good man, not one who would try to lure a woman away from her girlfriend.

Back to the other half of the party. Various plans for killing the ranger were proposed, but the requirement to make it look like the hit was set up by Lady Erdene complicated things. They suggested having Safi spread rumors, but those would take time to filter from Ashmont to Firth, and the whole point of the job was to buy horses so they could finish their quest more quickly.

Instead, they decided to take some identifiable clothes off one of Lady Erdene's rangers. Then they planned to disguise themselves – more discreetly than Khalil – to kill Helma. That way, the murder would be laid at her feet, instead of Lord Olros.

Lady Erdene's land – a town called Calhoun – was located near Firth. So Gavril and Zoja decided to make a small detour to pick up the disguise. Not knowing their plan in advance, I had to pull the next crisis out of my ass.

First, they lit a fire to attract a ranger, so I began with a survival-type roll for that. They wanted it seen, but they didn't want a fire so big that a ranger would run and get help. They only needed the one uniform and didn't want to fight an army of rangers wearing them. Next came an alertness roll to spot or hear the approaching ranger. The PCs wanted to ambush them, not the other way around.

Then I gave them a stealth check to hide – if they waited out in the open, they were going to get some penalties to take the ranger down because he would come with his sword drawn. And last was the ambush roll.

Bryan and Cedar did quite well on the crisis. A few of the rolls were a bit close because neither Gavril or Zoja emphasized mental stats, but they pulled it off – with some small bonuses from Danya, their little trainee mercenary – and ambushed Erdene's ranger. They gave his sword to Danya, who finally had her own full-sized weapon. Zoja took the ranger's crossbow so that she could conveniently drop it – in the hopes that it would be traced back to Erdene – and Gavril took the man's belt, which had a buckle with a stylized *E* for the Grove Lady's name.

I threw one extra thing into the scene. It wasn't quite part of the crisis, but I gave Zoja and Gavril some sanity damage. They just cold-bloodedly killed a man in the woods, and this wasn't even the guy they were paid to kill. He had done nothing wrong that they knew of – they just wanted his clothes. Bryan argued that Gavril is a professional assassin, but I countered that assassins are probably not very emotionally healthy people.

I also gave them a second, smaller sanity hit when they buried his corpse. Real friends may help friends move bodies, but they also take sanity damage together because that's a messed up thing to do.

Safi and Kaikoa's day went very differently, although it also involved rangers. Erica thought talking to them would be a good idea. Rangers travel all over the mountains and valleys, and if there were any place that might be protected from evils by the Sign, they may know of it. So Safi, Kaikoa and Alak'ai found a ranger bar which I named *The Ranger's Rest*.

But their lack of money struck again. No bartender was going to let Safi hang around all day without ordering anything, especially with a pair of Kels. Tydalus has got some bigotry between the Kelanua and inlanders, and it pissed Safi off.

Kaikoa had an idea to pitch their services as rat-catchers. He's got a predatory bird companion and a medieval fantasy world has a surplus of rats. Buuuuuut... business owners tend not to take kindly to implications that their establishments are infested with rats, so they got told off and then a back-handed offer to stick Safi's Kelanua friends down in front of the competition – The Leaky Keg – to drive away *their* business.

Safi just couldn't take the double-dose of bigotry, so she gave the Ranger's Rest bartender the finger and went over to The Leaky Keg. But not to screw with the owner there. Safi and Kaikoa did some rat-catching, but they released the animals into The Ranger's Rest instead and told the Keg's barkeep about it in hopes of being more well-received there.

Safi wasn't in the mood for any more bigotry, but even the Keg's nicer barkeep was uncomfortable with the two Kels. Alak said that their search was more important than his pride and volunteered to leave. Kaikoa decided he could entertain himself by making friends with another strange inlander animal – some stray dogs.

So that left Safi alone at The Leaky Keg, standing out front and warning passers-by about the rat problem at The Ranger's Rest. She brought in business for the Keg, including the rangers she wanted to talk to. Safi's built for talking her way out of trouble and those social skills were pretty applicable to the situation, so Erica rolled incredibly well drumming up business. Well enough that the Keg's barkeep decided to pay her.

Erica rolled a success in collecting stories from the rangers, too. But there were no clues pointing to the Sign, leaving Erica and Jack to conclude that they had to explore the peaks around Vanhome, the other major city in northern Korvath. Good thing that they're collecting money for horses.

Kaikoa and Alak'ai decided that they would hang out in front of The Ranger's Rest a little, just to make the bartender's own biases hurt him. Naturally, the barkeep didn't appreciate that and tried shooing the pair off, and I made Jack deal with the cranky Antoran man. Of the skill checks I offered, Jack opted for intimidation and rolled well enough to make the Rest's owner retreat, too fearful to send one of his regulars out to chase off the Kels.

Erica decided to spend the money Safi had earned on an inn room so that they wouldn't have to sleep in the woods again. It was money they might need for horses, but Erica was willing to trust in Safi's mad social skills and wanted to do something nice for her two Kelanua friends since her people have been treating them like shit.

She only had enough money for one room, but those mad negotiation skills haggled that into an inn room for Safi and the linen room for the Kels. She tried to give them the proper room, but the innkeeper refused. Alak and Kaikoa stopped Safi from turning that into another fight – besides, they could make hammocks with the sheets and if only the floor swayed, it would be just like sleeping on the ship. Safi relented. Hey, at least they were indoors. Sleeping in the woods without a fire wasn't anyone's idea of a good time.

Back to the other half of the party on the murder-mission. They found the rangers' favorite bar in Firth, The Old Stump, and lurked until they spotted Helma heading inside with her ranger buddies, then followed them in.

They took some seats nearby and Gavril did his impression of someone looking conspicuously inconspicuous. It was a weird-ass act they had to put on, pretending to be people trying to hide their identity while trying to make sure that they didn't hide it.

But when they attacked, Gavril aced the role to "accidentally" show his new Erdene-branded belt buckle before he could cover it, and Cedar actually asked if Zoja could purposefully take a hit that would break the crossbow's strap, so losing it would be believable. It's not often that a PC volunteers to take damage, so I let Zoja take some and she got to drop her weapon.

It was a weird and fun fight. The job was to kill Helma, because she betrayed her lord, but Olros didn't want half his rangers killed, so the mercenaries had to leave everyone else alive. They zeroed in on Helma and Cedar loved her axe-versus-axe battle just as much as I hoped, though Gavril ended up being the one to drop her with an arrow to the neck. Then they had to boogie before all the other rangers killed them.

I hit the mercenaries with some more sanity damage because they just killed a woman for money. Not much, though, since this was the job and she was a traitor. But killing isn't easy on the mind or soul. Only Gavril had to take the damage, though, because he did the actual killing. If Zoja had landed the killing blow, it would have been her.

But they regained all of their sanity with some shots of booze... Disturbingly realistic?

The mercenaries escaped and hid outside of Firth until things calmed down, then Gavril changed clothes and went back to meet their contact. Khalil's agent was at the rendezvous point and guided him back to The Old Stump. Khalil thanked Gavril – very publicly – for the warning of Erdene's treachery and said that it was too bad that his warning wasn't in time to save Helma.

Gavril didn't care what story Khalil wanted to tell so long as they got paid, but he gave all of the right responses and left with the reward.

The next day, the party all got back together in Ashmont. I was done bouncing back and forth between them and they had enough money to try to buy horses. Enough for one horse, actually...

The party is four player characters and two NPCs, so there's six people. They figured that they would need at least three horses to make it to Vanhome, so it was time for Safi to stand up and haggle her ass off.

And Erica rolled well. She came *really* close to talking the price of the horses down, but fell just a little short. So the party sorted through their inventories for anything that they could throw in to sweeten the deal and get them all three horses they needed.

I just didn't think that a horse-trader, with one of the most uncommon and expensive commodities in Korvath, wanted any used armor or weapons, bandages or alcohol. And that's all they owned. My players began to panic... Two horses weren't going to cut it.

Danya had jack shit, but Alak had his spyglass. He's a sailor and a stargazer. And Safi even managed not to steal it after all this time. So Alak'ai volunteered to sell the glass, since it was the only thing any of them owned worth a handful of salt.

I couldn't have known that Erica's roll would fall short. I actually kind of expected her to blow it out of the water, but it worked out perfectly. Safi's in this whole mess because her father's telescope got stolen and she tried to take it back. Now the man she's crushing on sacrifices his...

It was romantic story gold. If your games include love subplots, that is the kind of shit to look out for. I couldn't have planned it any better.

It was just enough to make up the last pounds and the party got their three horses. They split up to ride, pairing the smaller characters with the larger. So Danya rode with Zoja, Gavril with Kaikoa, and Safi with Alak'ai. I figured that I would be able to put them on a horse together, but next to the spyglass incident, that was chump change.

As soon as they stopped riding for the night, Safi pulled Danya aside to confess her temptation. She assured Danya that she loved her, that she was everything Safi had ever wanted in a woman... But admitted that Alak'ai was everything she ever wanted in a man.

Love triangle complete. Now we just need to see where it goes.

Vanhome

Session 9.

During setup for game this week – which involves starting the map tool on our laptops and seeing if anyone wants to spend their experience – Cedar said she filled in the cracks still left in Zoja's backstory. She had named Zoja's mother *Valtha* and decided that her fighting school taught a two-weapon style. Two axes like Zoja, or two swords, two cows, or paired whatevers.

I can vividly imagine Zoja's mother beating someone to death with a small cow in each hand.

But after that, the session had a rough start. Bryan was on call for work and dealt with three client issues that day. Jack had spent the morning at another horse show where he won two first-place ribbons, but left him tired. And Cedar was having a mean migraine, so it was going to be a bit of a slog to get everyone into character. But I hoped that if I could get them warmed up, we would get up to speed.

Danya was riding with Zoja, so I had her try to engage the older mercenary in conversation. Danya was familiar with Vanhome and suggested that Dunspire, being the northernmost town of the city-state – and the *only* one built up north of Vanhome – had colorful auroras in their skies, but hadn't been abandoned. Zoja just nodded and agreed that if Danya said so, then it was worth investigating.

Which let me segue into Danya asking Zoja if she was really serious about that prophetess stuff. She's not, right? Danya pointed out that she hasn't spoken in any tongues lately, fallen into trances, or even had any bad dreams. It was over and Danya was fine now. She can't foretell the future. But Zoja just shrugged and said that it doesn't mean Danya's not a prophetess.

While Cedar didn't engage with Danya much, I liked the scene because I got to frame her as recovered and healed. When Danya is taken by the cult in Dunspire and goes into her final spiral, I will reverse that. I get to unravel the players' work with her and wound their characters by impacting Danya.

But it was a pretty low-energy conversation and the game wasn't building up much momentum yet.

So I moved on to Erica, since she's my high-interaction player. During a break in riding, she and Danya talked a bit about Alak'ai, and Danya took a turn sharing a horse with him. Alak's kind and all of the other stuff Safi said he was. And while Danya might not have a particular soft spot for stargazing and Kelanua lore-songs, given her background, a kind man means the world to her.

Erica decided that since no one else is doing a romantic story arc, she's going to have all of the romances herself. She promoted her *who will she pick* love triangle into a new *I want them both* polyamorous one.

I considered and decided that Danya was game – as long as she didn't lose Safi – and the girls figured that they should let Alak'ai know that they were both interested. He had admitted to temptation with Safi, but they had to find out if he liked Danya.

Erica also wanted Safi to reveal to Alak that she spoke Kelanua. She hadn't gotten the chance to share that bit of information, and she wanted to apologize that he had to sell his spyglass to afford the horses. Safi said she owed him one, since it was the money that she had spent on the inn room that set them back.

Erica hadn't rehearsed what she wanted Safi to say, and trying to talk about language and telescopes and *oh, by the way, want to be in a three-way relationship with me and Danya?* didn't fit together very smoothly. Erica wasn't happy with her scene, but she's hard on herself that way.

I was glad that Erica was trying something new romantically – she's never tried a polyamorous relationship in game before – and Alak'ai readily agreed to get involved with the two Antoran women. But Erica was clearly having a hard time settling into her smooth-talking Safi groove.

Damn it, even my power-player was having a hard time today. What else could I do?

I had the players make some travel rolls. They had a long trip from Ashmont to Vanhome and time was the enemy, so a navigation check let them shave a few days off the route by taking lower passes that were open due to the low tide. I also had them make some ride checks since they're all new to horses. Zoja's the only one who even has the ride skill.

The cost of failure was just the loss of a little energy that they couldn't recover until they got to rest in an actual bed. Because we had travel time, everyone was full up on health, energy, and sanity, so it was a chance for me to take a little bite out of their resources, to soften them up for Dunspire.

Having the players make some rolls got everyone to put down their cell phones and pick up their dice, to look at their character sheets and engage a little. Now that I had their attention, I wanted to get them to Dunspire where I could put them on their toes and on the defensive.

But be careful hurrying your players. *Is there anything anyone wants to do on the journey?* is my standard check to see if they have scenes to play out. If no one does, then I can segue the travel.

Erica had one small scene. While Danya rode with Alak'ai, she was with Gavril and asked how Danya did on her first mercenary job. Danya had told Safi the details, but Safi wasn't as excited about ambushing and murdering a ranger for his belt as Danya seemed to be. When Safi had the chance to talk to Gavril, she wanted to know how mercenaries coped with that.

As far as how Danya did, Gavril simply said she made it through the fight alive. Most new mercenaries don't survive their first battle. Decent praise from Gavril. But when Safi asked how he coped with murder, Gavril just said he had been doing it all his life.

Erica had the opportunity to ask how that started – a chance for Gavril to bust out his backstory. Bryan was a little vague. He doesn't commit the details of his own backstory to memory, really. But he gave Safi the synopsis: some people came to collect a debt from his family and tried to hurt them, so he killed them. They kept sending people and he kept killing them until they stopped dispatching leg-breakers and sent a recruiter. He was fourteen.

Safi was horrified and asked how the hell he dealt with that. She was thinking of Danya, how to keep her soul from withering away in this job, and Gavril all but said he was dead inside, leaving Safi to worry. Bryan could have gone into greater detail or played it up for more impact, but it was a scene.

And no one else had anything, so we glossed over the next few days of riding and got the party to Dunspire.

I gave Cedar some local knowledge, mostly that northern towns tend to build on the east, west, or south side of the peaks to keep the view of the aurora to a minimum. Dunspire was the only village north of Vanhome.

Erica asked if Safi had ever read about it and I gave her a history check. Being one of the skills Safi excels at, Erica smoked that roll, so I told her that Dunspire was built by the Antoran refugees when their population swelled past the limits of Vanhome and its older towns.

Erica made the correct logical leap that if Dunspire was built by Antorans, that the peak it occupied might have been avoided by the Cthyans, another one of their hints about the Sign.

But then Cedar's headache jumped up another notch. She said she was going to crash on the spare couch, so we ended up with an unplanned break. We gave her about half an hour and then I asked Bryan to check up on her. Cedar was conked out, though, and not up for more game.

I knew that we had some investigation coming up in Dunspire. Safi would want to talk to people and ask questions like she did in Ashmont, so I thought we could get away with doing some scenes that Zoja would probably remain quiet during, anyway. We want to finish this game before the holidays, when everybody gets really busy. So I decided to mush on.

The characters decided that since Dunspire is their best lead, they would pass up Vanhome and go straight there. We all agreed that Zoja wouldn't have any problems with that. Zoja's not exactly the sentimental type who would want to race back home to visit her mercenary-mommy while they were in the neighborhood.

While a stop in Vanhome would have been good to demonstrate the character of a typical city-state – one I could use for contrast – Ashmont did that job and I'm not trying to milk this game for every scene. We're already weeks over my original estimated run-time.

So as they neared Dunspire, the party got their first look at the distant aurora. My players all knew that the aurora – like the sea – was something bad and all said their characters tried not to look. Hmm, then how about an alertness check, but with all their special heightened senses bonuses as a penalty instead? Kaikoa in particular had some character attributes that made his alertness checks truly badass. A successful roll meant that the character got to put their eyes somewhere safe, while a failed one meant too much of a glimpse of the aurora.

There were some failures and then some checks to resist sanity damage. It was just a glimpse and the aurora was far away, but I got to start on the creepy vibe and begin whittling away the characters' sanity.

My players were in just the right mood when I described their approach to Dunspire. The needle-sharp mountain, the weathered and patchy city wall, the claustrophobically close-set buildings, the wary looks of the townsfolk. My players took all of two seconds to assume this place was dangerous and there was something wrong with the whole town.

Perfect.

Player characters are far more paranoid than most people in the real world. They know they're playing a game, and that their job is to fight antagonists, so they look for them everywhere. My group knows that we're playing a Lovecraft-themed horror game, and that quaint, isolationist towns with fish-eyed inhabitants are bad news, so they have reasons to be wary that their characters don't. There's a certain amount of unavoidable meta-gaming going on here.

But you know what? If players are paranoid, they are engaged. They ask questions. They want to make alertness and investigation checks to look at everything, then cringe at what they find. What I kicked off by ramping up the creepy factor, my players ran with.

I'll take that trade any day. It makes it a little harder for me to sneak up on the group, to spring the ambushes that I have planned. They won't trust anyone here in Dunspire and won't let down their guard, but it's worth it to have them on their toes and being active.

Despite the paranoia, they decided to split the party. Safi took the two Kelanua boys again, and then headed to the church to ask about stories that might hold more clues. Just like in Ashmont. And also as in the last city, the mercenaries were going to check out the taverns.

Awesome! They're doing the same investigation and research as they did in Ashmont, so I get to highlight just how different Dunspire is. They're going to compare everything here to the last place, which makes it easy for me to give Dunspire its own character and to make even slight differences stand out.

Since Cedar was still zonked out, I started with Safi and Kaikoa investigating the church. They went in and I gave them some alertness and investigation rolls. Safi didn't get much, but Kaikoa did amazingly well – I told you that he was good at those checks – so he got all the little "off" details.

The murals on the walls showed ocean waves swallowing whole cities, but there were no images of Zelleny and Rhystar holding the water back. There weren't any statues of Zelleny or Rhystar at all, actually. And the cities seemed to have strange architecture, even for inlander dwellings. And, of course, there was the locked doors in the back, leading to the inner sanctum.

Kaikoa whispered all this to Safi in Kelanua, pointing out what was missing compared to the church in Ashmont. And Jack remembered enough about the Ashmont church that he actually pounced on the differences. He hurried to point it all out to Safi before the priest could even greet them.

The priest was welcoming and polite, and I borrowed a hint of the same accent that Cedar uses for Zoja. And almost because of his politeness, Erica and Jack were immediately on edge. Both of their characters spoke Kelanua, so they got to talk privately right in front of the priest. Safi gave a story about writing a book and asked lots of questions. Safi didn't ask about the Sign at first – she just wondered about the strange cities.

"Oh, you know artists," the priest answered. "They didn't have your Miskatonic history books and can hardly be blamed for their wild imaginations when it came to the cities of our lost ancestors."

Plausible. So Safi asked why there weren't any images of Rhystar and Zelleny.

"In our sect of Zelletar, we believe that like Orvo, Zelleny and Rhystar shall return from the sea one day," was the answer. "And their sacred images remain lost until they return."

Also plausible. What about Zelleny's star, one of their symbols?

"Not all sects of Zelletar believe that she followed a star," the priest said. "I'm afraid we are one of them."

That also made a bit of sense. Everything the priest said made just enough sense and could explain why his church was off... But that just made Erica and Jack *more* paranoid.

Safi asked if they had any other symbols or *signs* for their sect, and Erica and Jack asked for rolls to gauge the priest's reaction. They both did well so they caught just the slightest facial tic at the mention. Nothing concrete, nothing like evidence, but just enough to keep them on the edge of paranoia.

They backed out of there quickly. Safi didn't think she was going to get anything out of the priest, nothing true anyway, and anything that might be interesting was behind the doors of the members-only inner sanctum. Which Kaikoa instantly wanted to break into.

I switched over to the mercenary half of the group. Gavril took Danya, but didn't go straight to a tavern. He wanted to find someone homeless and desperate, someone who would tell them all about the town for a few pounds. But Dunspire's a small village, not big enough for slums. The whole place wasn't exactly rich, but there didn't seem to be anyone who lived on the streets. Bryan found that suspicious, so good. You'll see how quickly they found *everything* suspicious in Dunspire.

By now, everyone's paranoia was self-perpetuating. I just got the players to put on their murder-colored glasses. They saw everything through that filter of mistrust without me actually having to do very much. Set the mood right and your players will do all the work of creeping themselves out.

About this time, I remembered the horses. The party had three and they can't take them into taverns and churches, plus they were expensive and hard to get. So since Cedar was asleep in the office, we had Zoja stay with the mounts in the town square to guard them while the others looked around. Since she's the only character with the ride skill, it even made some logical sense.

I also left Alak'ai with Zoja. He was the other big, well-armed character and the players all wanted their most intimidating people keeping the horses safe. No one wanted them to get horse-napped. And Alak had been silent during the visit to the church, so moving him seemed like a good idea.

There are two things I want to note about that decision. One, the reason I kept Alak'ai quiet at the church was because Jack and Erica were really hyped up by the creepy murals and the missing holy stuff. Kaikoa had an almost non-stop string of warnings and Jack loved speaking Kelanua right in front of the priest, giving Safi ammunition for her questions and suspicions.

When my players are running with some piece of the story, they really don't need my NPCs butting in. I didn't want to have Alak'ai comment on a single thing because it would have been one less thing for Kaikoa to talk about – and he was talking to Safi about *everything*.

I'd also like to point out that we decided to place Alak with the horses *after* the church scene. I forgot about the horses, so we didn't stick Alak and Zoja with them until afterward. Players rarely mind that kind of minor mistake. Alak had been silent in the church, and it was easy for everyone to retcon his location. (If you're not familiar with the term, *retcon* means to make retroactively canon.)

When I'm really on the ball, we don't have to retcon anything, but it happens sometimes and no one minds. And they retcon stuff, too. Hell, Zoja's backstory didn't exist when we began game. Cedar and I have been slowly developing it and working it into Zoja as we go. So don't be afraid to admit to a mistake and correct it.

Back to the game! Eventually, Gavril did go to a tavern, choosing the poorer and rougher of the two in Dunspire. I think that he was still looking for someone fallen on hard times, someone he could get talking by buying them an ale.

Instead, Gavril walked into the tavern of a remote, isolationist town where everyone knows everybody else, no one likes strangers, and there's the distinct possibility that any of them may have fish-men in their ancestry.

I put on my best grumpy face and responded to Gavril's questions with sullen silence. When the bartender *did* answer, he used only a few grumbling, thickly-accented words. Gavril asked if there was an inn – to which the answer was *yes* – then finished his ale and left without trying to talk to anyone else.

So Bryan didn't engage in a lot of conversation. You may have noticed that he doesn't do much of that. But Bryan was asking for all sorts of rolls to size people up, check them out, and asking me for every little detail. The tavern didn't have a sign or even a name, and though I told him that Dunspire is small enough that it only has two (*the tavern* and *the other tavern*) and they don't need signs, Bryan wanted to know if he'd seen *any* writing in the town. I'm not sure what the level of literacy in Dunspire had to do with anything, but my player was sifting the place through a fine mesh screen, so I answered his questions.

Bryan might not have been very talkative, but he was engaged, which is even better. And I played Danya as the junior mercenary, asking Gavril why this or that was suspicious so Bryan could explain his investigation as I squeezed a little dialogue out of him.

Gavril checked out the inn next and got pretty much the same treatment. The inn houses travelers, so it pretty much exists for the use of outsiders, but I made the innkeeper as reluctant about it as she could possibly be. Zoja was the only one with any money left, though, so as soon as Gavril determined that there were rooms to rent, he backed out of there with promises to bring his friends.

Promises that he didn't intend to keep. Bryan found some of the abandoned homes down at the tide line, the kind that flood when the Grandfather tide rolls in to turn the mountains into islands, and planned to get the group to stay in Hotel Dank instead.

The two halves of the party met back up with Zoja and Alak'ai in the square, and there was relief from both sides to be reunited. They traded stories, where Kaikoa and Gavril gleefully shared how dangerous and wrong they thought Dunspire was. Gavril suspected that the locals were hiding something, and Jack wanted Kaikoa and Gavril to break into the town church's inner sanctum. He didn't even particularly think the Sign was there, he just knew that it was secret and the locals were closed-off. Which only made Jack want to know even more.

But that's the sort of decision that should be made by the entire group. And the characters had to decide if they were going to brave the Dunspire inn or sleep in some damp, drafty abandoned houses, but Cedar's pain level was too high to get her back in and continue playing.

So we'll do that next week. Still, we got a decent-sized game in and actually went through more of my outline than in the last two or three sessions, so I was happy with our progress.

You may have noticed there wasn't a fight in this week's session. Last week, the mercenaries murdered Helma... But the week before that? No combat, and I don't think I even ran any crises. But everyone had a good time and my players were engaged, despite the slow start to the day.

I like to emphasize the role-playing part of RPGs and if we have a game session with lots of role-playing but no combat, we're okay with that. Cedar is the most bored during a fight – though Zoja is really tearing all my usual Cedar-isms to pieces.

But if your group wants to throw down more, bandits waylaying travelers through the passes are always great. With the historically low tide, there are new routes open that robbers would love to stake out before the competition. You could make sure your group passes through Vanhome and get your PCs involved in a pride-duel or two.

All they have to do is bump into somebody on the street or look at someone wrong, Vanhome is chock full of people looking to make a name for themselves. Or you could have some drunken Dunspire villagers start a fight with the outsiders. There are ways to add fights if your group needs them – but if they don't, then move on to the role-playing.

Curse Your Sudden But Inevitable Betrayal

Session 10.

Players are suspicious bastards. Everyone was feeling better this week and we got right into game. My players were already primed to take on Dunspire. They opted to stay at the inn after all because they knew that they were going to have penalties on their rest and healing if they slept in a crumbling shack. And they knew they were going to be breaking into the church at some point, so they wanted to have to sneak through less of the town.

Safi haggled some cheap inn rooms, then Zoja arranged a watch on their horses, and everyone sat down for dinner. The innkeeper served porridge and they acted like she had offered them a severed head. No one wanted to touch the food or wine at first.

Eventually, Cedar decided that Zoja doesn't care and isn't afraid, so she had a bowl. Safi isn't as paranoid as her player is, and Erica had her eat, too. Then I gave them both an alertness check to see if they tasted anything off. Erica got a critical failure and Cedar rolled a normal failure. So I just told them it tasted bad.

There was absolutely nothing in the shitty porridge. No poison, no sleeping potion, nothing sinister. Well, maybe some rat crap. But having to make a roll – even if I was just messing with them – only confirmed all my players' suspicions. Bryan and Jack watched Safi and Zoja, just waiting for them to keel over.

But that wasn't the plan. I let them arrange their watch rotation, which gave me an opportunity to place Danya outside on her own, guarding the horses. I suddenly didn't have to worry about any of the players derailing my plans by rescuing her during the crisis.

Not that the escape from the inn crisis went exactly as planned. When the people of Dunspire rushed their rented rooms, Zoja was tempted to just charge in and start hacking the whole village to pieces. But Cedar thought that an inn full of bloodthirsty townsfolk might be a bit much, even for Zoja, and decided to barricade the door and then escape out the window with the rest of the party.

Except for Gavril. While everybody else was grabbing their gear and climbing out the window, Bryan wanted to light up a candle – and then the whole room.

What's the roll for lighting a candle? I've never made anyone roll dice for something so simple before. That would be like asking a player for an athletics check to tie their shoes. But I couldn't deny that lighting a candle quickly with angry villagers trying to kick in the door required a skill check and consequences.

I went with a mental stat and nature check, which is what I had made Bryan use during the crisis with the ranger back in Ashmont. But it wasn't really a candle that he wanted – Gavril needed an open flame to burn the whole place down. So I gave Bryan an arson roll, which went well – especially since I gave him a bonus per dose of alcohol he wanted to spend dousing the room.

Needless to say, the room went up in flames.

But Gavril's extra crisis steps threw a bit of a monkey wrench into things. Everyone else went out the window, climbing up to the roof, and now I had players at different stages of the escape crisis. I was saved somewhat by Safi, who wanted to know where Danya was and wasn't going to leave without her. So I gave Erica some rolls to spot Danya – as well as their horses – all being taken away across the town square. Then I had her dodge stones and firewood hurled at her while she stood there searching.

That let Gavril catch up and then the rest of the crisis went as planned. They did have to convince Safi that the villagers obviously wanted Danya alive, and that they also needed to be alive if they intended to save her. Safi was hysterical, but Erica let Alak throw her over his shoulder and leave without a fight.

And then – without any prompting – the party holed up in the abandoned houses on the lowest terrace of Dunspire. They bound their wounds and plotted their rescue just like I hoped.

The characters opted for a stealthy approach, but with a slightly arson-y distraction. They went down to the tavern that Gavril and Danya investigated, broke in and stole some booze. I gave Gavril a roll to see how much he could take without losing a lot of time – they were in a hurry to get Danya back. Then he lit the place on fire.

Kaikoa wanted a piece of the arson action and lit up a barrel of whiskey, then rolled his impromptu Falspire firebomb – I modified *Molotov cocktail* for Tydalus – down the hill. I guess they didn't like the inn that much. The party gave it one flaming barrel on Yelp.

Church Picnic

I let the players create a pool of bonus points with their arson distraction roll. They divided the points up between them as a bonus to their stealth rolls. And thanks to that bump, everyone succeeded in their checks and made it to the church.

The player characters all got inside and then opened the doors to the sanctum, though my description of runes carved along the edges freaked them out and kept them sitting there debating until they got worried that some townsfolk would come by. But the runes were just flavor text, and nothing happened when the characters went through.

The Inner Sanctum

Everybody hurried into the next room. When they spotted Danya mumbling in a dreamy trance and surrounded by masked cultists, they forgot about stealth and charged right in. At the last moment, I decided to throw some townsfolk in with the cultists since the PCs never ended up fighting any through all the crises. I wanted to use those enemies because it's creepy having someone's grandma try to kill you with her knitting needles.

But the characters were pretty murder-tastic and didn't lose any of their weapons while escaping the inn, so they were armed – and not opposed to cutting down any creepy grandmas that got between them and Danya.

They handled the fight well, as usual, but there were a couple of wrinkles. The priest and his magic hit Zoja *hard*. Swing a sword at her and my chances of an enemy actually connecting are pretty low. Plus, she's got enough armor and health to take it even if I do. But throwing some magic at Zoja bloodied her nose, and did a number on her sanity at the same time. With magic and the scary statue at the center of the sanctum, Zoja took a *lot* of sanity damage.

Gavril was hurling knives and shooting arrows at the priest with a vengeance, but Bryan had the most terrible luck. Either the priest defended each attack or Gavril rolled a critical failure.

Safi also had a rough time. She ran into an alcove and then held her actions, hoping that the cultists would swarm Zoja so she could run around them and get to Danya. I gave her a roll to look non-threatening, but despite being a social check that played to all of her strengths, Erica didn't do well enough. Some cultists went after Safi and blocked the alcove, trapping her there.

It took Safi and Kaikoa a few rounds to kill or move the cultists out of the way so she could reach Danya. And when she did, Safi didn't just want to smack the priest with her staff – she was there to shake Danya out of her trance. I gave Erica an empathy check (with a bonus because Danya and Safi are romantically involved) and she managed to shout the girl awake, so I unlocked Danya's bonus.

With Danya and her NPC bonus back in play, and the crowd of cultists beginning to thin, the PCs quickly turned the tide of battle.

They stacked up a massive combo on the priest and then dropped him with it.

The looming, betentacled statue chipped away at the PC's sanity all through the fight, and then while Gavril cracked the safe. I don't know why I used a combination lock instead of one that could be opened with a key like in the notes. But as soon as I said *safe*, Bryan grinned and wanted to bust it open.

I had the priest clinging to life, but rather than ask him to open it up, Gavril did the deed. Actually, when the priest *did* try to talk to them, ranting about the Elder Sign, Gavril just re-stabbed him.

When they got the safe open, Kaikoa grabbed the stone marked with the Elder Sign. Jack was happy to stop taking sanity damage, but Bryan was less pleased, since Gavril's sanity was down in single digits. And collecting some of his thrown knives nearly earned our not-so-friendly neighborhood assassin a new derangement.

But the players all reasoned that their characters didn't understand just how the Sign – which they now knew as the Elder Sign, thanks to Danya and the priest – worked, and didn't have cause to pass it around right now. And Bryan managed to get Gavril out of there before his brain dribbled out his ears.

You Are Now Leaving Dunspire

On their way out of the church, Kaikoa checked the rooms off the inner sanctum hallway. He found the robes and cultists' masks, and grabbed some disguises. The characters were all beat up badly enough that they didn't want to fight their way out of Dunspire.

But in disguise, they were able to bluff their way past the townsfolk outside, claiming the strangers were dealt with. They relieved the guards who took their horses, then walked their mounts away. The PCs claimed that the priest wanted the horses moved to the farming terrace to graze, and Safi's awesome social skills ensured that all their bluffs worked.

Once they got through the city gate, though, they mounted up and rode like Rhystar!

Their words, not mine, and I was pleased they were using terms like that. My players are absorbing the world lore nicely.

And that wrapped up Chapter 3 of game. Which is a good thing, since Jack is starting college soon and we've got less than a month left before he moves across the state.

Chapter 4 is pretty short... but this entire game was *supposed* to be short, and just look how long it's run. Erica has played out most of what can be done with her intersecting romantic arcs, though, and the rest aren't usually high-interaction players, so I can probably segue through a lot of the travel. But I'll certainly be looking to move the chapter along so we can finish up this campaign before Jack heads away to school.

CHAPTER 4

Session II.

During the downtime, I was talking with Erica, as my Costoryteller and coauthor, about how Tydalus was going. And for the most part, the answer was *good*.

My only lament was that I expected there to be more derangements by now. Gavril was the only one with any, and he just has the post-traumatic stress disorder. But to be fair to myself, I did drive Zoja insane early in the game, even if she lucked out with a critical success that let her buy it off not long after.

But we took a look at our sanity mechanics, which we just made for Tydalus. They're a first draft and if I got to run this game again, they could use a second brush-up pass. Erica and I decided that the alcohol and dreamcap restored too much sanity when used during downtime. The PCs just filled their sanity back up too easily. So we would cut the restorative part of the drugs in half. It was too late to do anything about it now, but if we ever use the sanity mechanic again, we can refine it.

Or *is* it too late? Erica gave me a great idea. I hand out a reward at the end of every chapter. Why not a chapter defect?

Yes! I'll give them each a defect called *Seen Too Much* that halves the amount of sanity restoration from drugs. There's only a single chapter left, so my players won't have to put up with it for long. And their characters still have all the travel time to get the normal, if slow, healing. But it just might let me keep them low enough that their final encounters will tip them into a derangement or two, and I don't have to wait for another game to try it out.

When I handed out the defect to everyone at the beginning of this week's session, they all groaned... and then readily agreed that it was perfect. And to make it up to them, I restored a little sanity for burning half of Dunspire down. That place was evil, and they hurt that evil. That's good for the soul.

Pursuit

I started this week's game with an NPC cutscene back in Dunspire. The lord-mayor walked through the ash-covered town and stepped over the bodies in the church. When a surviving cultist informed him that the outsiders had escaped, the mayor told them to prepare for a summoning.

I haven't done any cutscenes (scenes that are entirely narrated and include none of the player characters) in Tydalus, but I put one in here. The PCs are about to be hunted down by the Byakha and I'd like the players – if not their characters – to know where the hell it came from.

After escaping Dunspire, Bryan had Gavril dose up with some dreamcap. He took two hits, which was enough for him to suffer a penalty on the dice. The players have been careful not to give their characters enough drugs to get a penalty except when they have a lot of downtime, but for once I have a PC drugged up when there's rolls to make. I was excited.

They were just the usual riding rolls that I've been having them make, but with the dreamcap penalty, Bryan failed. And the energy loss penalty for failing brought Gavril almost down to zero. At zero, a character falls unconscious. And when the man who's steering the horse passes out on a switchback mountain trail, people might fall off cliffs.

Kaikoa was the one riding with Gavril, so Jack got a few rolls to take control of the horse and to stop their drugged-up assassin from slumping out of the saddle. I made him choose which one Kaikoa was going to prioritize – the second roll got a penalty.

Jack chose to save the horse first. After all, if their mount slipped and stepped off the road, then the horse, Gavril and Kaikoa would all fall together. Besides, Kaikoa's better at the athletics roll I gave him to grab Gavril, and might actually make it with the penalty.

And he did. Jack managed to rein up the horse and keep Gavril from falling. They decided to tie Gavril into the saddle so the group could keep riding, and it resulted in some more impromptu world-building.

Alak'ai ordered Kaikoa to secure Gavril in place with a drunk knot. I decided that in the Kelanua lighthouses, when you're going to get drunk, you tie yourself to something sturdy with a knot that you have to be sober to untie. That way you can't drunkenly fall down all the stone staircases or walk off a balcony two thousand feet in the air.

I added a few other details to the pursuit, too. I had the shadow of the Byakha pass over the group, describing its creepy shape and how it moves. Byakha can fly via an alien organ called a *hune*, rather than with its wings, so it doesn't move like a bird. My description foreshadowed the attack and kept the players' paranoia at a boil.

Next, I had the party spot a campfire. I had talked about how the low tide opened up new mountain passes, uncharted roads that bandits liked to target. But other than Gavril and Zoja's first intro-ductory scene, I haven't used any actual bandits against the group during their travels. Tydalus was supposed to be a short game and we're already on a deadline, so I didn't want any extra fights, espe-cially against something as prosaic as human bandits.

But since I've mentioned the bandit problems, there have to be bandits. And I had a use for them other than combat.

Kaikoa is a scout, so he headed out to do some actual scouting. And since Gavril's got the stealth chops, too, he went along for the ride. And they found a bandit camp that had been torn to pieces.

Kaikoa wanted to inspect the bodies, of course. Good, because the bandits had been badly mangled. They were clawed to bits, and looked like they had fallen off a lighthouse or a cliff. But they were scattered around a meadow in the lowlands. What was there to fall off of? Jack and Bryan instantly connected this carnage to the flying shadow they saw earlier.

Both Kaikoa and Gavril also took some sanity damage from the hideous violence of the scene, and they didn't even stop to loot the corpses. There were weapons there, armor – if they felt like hosing the guts off – and there could have been food or even money. But no, they wanted to get away, back to the group, and to move everyone under cover *right now*.

So my players weren't surprised by the Byakha's attack, though they found the description of the creature nicely disturbing. The battle with it went quickly and straightforward. I only changed one thing from the notes – I doubled the Byakha's health. The player characters kick a lot of ass now and with only one target for them all to pile onto, the original stats weren't going let it last long. And they stacked their combo abilities on the Byakha, then crushed it in two rounds anyway.

Afterward, they hurried away and then stopped for the night in Calhoun. You may remember it as the place where the mercenaries ambushed a ranger, killed him, and buried the body in the woods.

Good times.

Thanks to Safi's bargaining power, they got to rest in an actual inn room. Danya had sat out part of the Byakha battle, just as outlined in my game notes. So Safi wanted to know what Danya meant when she said that it was "only ordinary matter." In answer, I had Danya mix confusion with some rantings about great powers which straddle planes and span dimensions. Safi's a smart girl, but that went way over her head.

Safi left Danya safe with Alak'ai, then went down the hall to see Gavril, where she asked for some of the extracted dreamcap venom.

Erica tried to engage Bryan in some dialogue, asking how Gavril coped and if he and Zoja ever... you know... comforted each other.

Sex. She meant sex. Did Gavril and Zoja ever sleep together?

Bryan kept his answers to that pretty monosyllabic, so it was a short scene. And if you're curious, the answer was *no*. Gavril and Zoja don't knock armored boots.

Speaking of which... While dealing with romantic plot lines, the intimate scenes should generally remain off-camera. But right now, I needed Danya's sanity to be spinning out of control, and her relationship with Safi and Alak'ai gave me the hook I wanted.

My players were all instantly suspicious when I began narrating – in *non-explicit* terminology – the trio of lovers' nightly activities. Safi learned the three Cthyan dialects after reading the Azif, so she understood when Danya started screaming out for the blessing of Nyarlathotep and giving thanks to the Black Goat of the Woods.

Actually, the Black Goat of the Woods is Shub-Niggurath, not Nyarlathotep, but can you blame me for mixing up those weird-ass names when I have to pull some unhinged dialogue out of my butt? Safi panicked and the players were all creeped out, and that's what's important.

Alak and Safi made sure Danya slept with the Elder Sign under her pillow for the rest of the night. It calmed her, but didn't stop her strangeness.

Return to The Nautilus

I didn't have any other scenes for the ride back to The Nautilus, and other than keeping a nervous eye on Danya, neither did the players. The overland journey passed quickly and we got them back to the old Kelanua lighthouse.

Alak'ai was in his element again and back in charge. He rushed off to prep the *Iron Eel* and left Kaikoa to figure out something to do with the horses. Gavril and Zoja decided that a horse for each of them was part of their pay and Kaikoa agreed. He sold the third horse at the quartermarket (the name we gave to the place where Kelanua barter), then left the other two at the lighthouse. Putting the animals on their ship would have been difficult, and if Zoja and Gavril survived, they could claim them when this was all done.

I didn't want to make it too easy for the characters to gear up again, so I planned on raising the cost of all supplies. Everything's being shipped to The Hunter to hold off the Tekeli, so prices going up make sense. But everyone thought they had enough alcohol and didn't buy anything else.

Alak'ai gathered everyone back up from the lighthouse to get the *Iron Eel* on the move. I guess I did a good job showing Alak'ai's awkwardness during the inland chapter because they all noted how much more comfortable he was back onboard his own ship. When my players comment on that kind of thing and call it out before I do, that's how I know I played an NPC right.

But that was a good stopping point for the session. I think we've got a solid chance of finishing next week. We've got the return trip south, the crisis to get past the Tekeli, a fight against Dekara, then the temple scene.

That's it! Unless, of course, I decide to throw in a new scene or the players have anything else that they want to run. Have my projections about how long this game will go *ever* been right?

Race to the Temple

Session 12.

I was at a friend's birthday party earlier this week and telling him about Tydalus over dinner, about how I thought that I would have dished out a few more derangements by now. Cedar was there at the party, too. She overheard me talking and said she was pretty sure that the sanity situation would result in some more derangements soon.

Now, I had thought all the travel time was going to mean that everyone's sanity would be fine again by the time they reached the Tekeli, but Cedar pointed out that Zoja's sanity recovery was still going to leave her dangerously low. Especially with the penalties for sleeping in armor.

Sleeping in armor? On the *Iron Eel*? As the Storyteller, I know there's going to be some quiet travel because I don't have the time for another monster, and I don't like random combats. I prefer my encounters to have purpose. But the players don't know my plan. Not even Erica, who helped me develop the plot of this game, but didn't read my final outline.

"Yeah, and the sea is *so* safe," Cedar added sarcastically.

My players are still afraid. They're still paranoid. I may not have given their characters very many derangements, but I've certainly inflicted some on the players. So I'm heading into what will likely be the last game with some confidence that I've successfully established an atmosphere of terror and madness. Hell yeah!

That weekend, I recapped the last game as usual, then got the party setting out. Gavril, Zoja, and Kaikoa resumed training Danya during the day. At night, Danya had Safi and Alak'ai. So for her, life was pretty damn good. Which I used to contrast rising tensions on the *Iron Eel*.

The crew lost their original captain – Nakhona – and suffered terrible losses on the island. Then Alak'ai took over leadership, and they sailed off on a mysterious quest, where their captain, first mate and some inlanders all vanished into the mountains for weeks, and then came back with... a rock.

Can you blame the *Iron Eel* crew for not feeling very safe?

Jack did fine with his rolls picking up the crew's mood, but not as well overhearing their muttering. All Kaikoa caught was "Should we kill them?"

I had a whole bit with the sailors discussing if they should just throw the inlanders overboard or if they needed to actually take out their captain, too, but that's all Jack got. He caught enough to know there was trouble, though, which was what I needed.

I wanted the crew to have a realistic reaction to all the strangeness – if the PCs are paranoid, then the NPCs should be, too – and wanted to give Kaikoa another shot at doing some first mate stuff. I don't think Jack was excited about tackling the problem, though, or maybe he wasn't sure how to handle it.

He told Safi that the crew was unhappy and staring daggers at both the inlanders and their captain, then told her to warn Alak. Safi did – she doesn't want the man or the woman she loves being tossed into the sea – but I wasn't going to let Kaikoa off the hook yet.

Jack had Kaikoa move from his own cabin back into the crew quarters in a show of solidarity, like he did before. And he identified the same sailor stirring the shit as back in Chapter 1 – a woman named Varona. She has wanted to chuck Danya and Zoja both overboard since day one, and Varona's only become more enthusiastic about that idea.

Jack decided to talk to Varona, and she laid out the crew's problems for Kaikoa. Needless to say, she wasn't thrilled that all of this was about a rock. Jack *really* tried to sell the Elder Sign as a major accomplishment, but then he stuck his foot in his mouth. Varona brought up the sea-eyed women and Kaikoa... sort of promised her that the inlanders would get off the ship at The Hunter.

Well, that wasn't likely to happen. The mercenaries are in this until the Tekeli is gone, and Danya's probably going to stay with Alak'ai and Safi for... well, for as long as she can, depending upon how this story ends.

Jack didn't devote a lot of Kaikoa's build to diplomacy skills, so his rolls didn't exactly smooth everything over. Kaikoa waited until the crew was all asleep, then slipped out to tell Alak'ai how things were going. Again, I wasn't going to let him pass the buck.

For one thing, if the crew was unhappy with their captain and the captain tried to tackle that head-on, things might get really ugly.

And what exactly were Alak'ai's choices? Bend for the crew and try to make them happy, or take the hard line and shout them all into compliance? That kind of obedience is fragile and given that they're sailing into the Tekeli, it might break under the pressure.

And the other reason is that Alak's a non-player character. I try not to make problems that an NPC can solve. Even if this was an issue that Alak'ai *should* address himself, it's my job to come up with a reason that a PC will have to deal with it. Because it doesn't matter if Alak is the captain – this story is about Kaikoa, Safi, Gavril and Zoja. They're the main characters, the protagonists, and they're the ones who should be solving the problems.

So Alak'ai listened to Kaikoa, but then lobbed the problem right back to him. Captain-crew relations were the first mate's job. Alak knows – that was his job before this one. He suggested that Kaikoa show their crew the Elder Sign, to let them hold it and feel its effect.

Danya had been keeping the Sign as an anti-batshit device, but gave it up to ensure that the crew didn't mutiny. Besides, Danya told Safi after Kaikoa left that she had to give it up. She was scared to... The Elder Sign prevented Danya from being strange, but they didn't know how to use it against the Tekeli yet. Danya *needed* her strangeness to learn that. Safi and Alak didn't like it, but agreed.

So the next day, Kaikoa took the Elder Sign to Varona and rolled better to reassure her. But I set a threshold of success to quell the mutiny before things got ugly and let Jack know he was still a little short. Erica reminded Jack that the Kelanua keep an oral tradition and suggested Kaikoa make a song about their quest – one with a good unite-or-die moral.

Jack remembered that Zoja criticized Gavril some weeks before for telling a story about their mercenary work without any exciting detail. She wants to be remembered in verse. So Kaikoa hit Zoja up for some advice on his song.

Zoja had some really good advice for him! She told Kaikoa that the quest was too long and complex if he wanted to make a point.

And they all ran away from Dunspire, which wasn't exactly heroic. Plus, their enemies in the church were only human. What they all faced now was much, much worse.

But the Byakha... now *that* was a monster, like the Tekeli. They fought and beat it together, Antorans and Kelanua. And Zoja also said, of course, that the best songs are sung in taverns, when everyone's drunk enough to overlook the embellishments.

Safi volunteered her alcohol – I said that I would grant a bonus for each dose of liquor they spread around the crew – and then the players rolled to compose their song. Which Safi did most of the work on, since she actually had the art skill and spoke Kelanua.

With a hefty booze bonus and another from Safi's songwriting, Jack absolutely smoked the roll. Kaikoa spent the night in the crew quarters passing around bottles and singing about kicking some monster ass with the inlanders.

He did such a damned good job that I decided to give everyone some bonuses on the upcoming sailing crisis. The crew is primed to work together again, even with the inlanders. I also gave Zoja some sanity back. Being immortalized in song is her life's goal. It should give her some peace and satisfaction.

The players wanted to capitalize on the sense of unity, so I gave them some rolls to get some more speed out of the ship and crew. Hey, if they want to go faster and cut their recovery time short, why should I stop them?

But I had to give them the last knowledge they needed to end things. So Danya woke Alak and Safi screaming from a nightmare in which she witnessed an ancient, inhuman race making a sacrifice to activate the sign. All three got dressed and immediately brought the party together to discuss the sacrifice.

Zoja instantly rejected the "children" – Kaikoa, Safi, and Danya – as possible sacrifices. Alak'ai agreed, since he was rather attached to the party's three younger members. I didn't have him volunteer, though. Not yet, not unless Gavril and Zoja both refused, too.

But in the end, I didn't need Alak'ai at all. Zoja didn't hesitate to offer her life.

"You'll do it?" she asked Gavril.

"I remember my promise," he said.

Is that from the real story of how they met? They never told the whole story – or the same partial story – so we don't know.

But we were never meant to hear the whole history, or the true story of Gavril and Zoja. And dropping that fragment at this moment was perfect. Bryan pulled some promise out of his butt and dropped it into a serious scene. That gave it ten times more weight than if one of the other PCs just got Gavril drunk and asked him what really happened when they met.

It was great and no one argued Zoja's choice.

They drove the *Iron Eel* hard, so there was a certain momentum to the chapter. My players had the bit in their teeth and they were gunning for the end of the story. Which meant that I completely forgot to have some of the Kelanua sailors take their own lives while the Tekeli was chasing their ship, gibbering and screaming.

That's okay. Kaikoa had done so well with that song that I don't think the story lost anything without those suicides, and I didn't want to undo all of my players' work.

The *Iron Eel* charged right into the sailing crisis and there were no surprises there. The crisis did deal some damage and they had to spend a few of their re-rolls to make it through intact. Which just means they won't have them for what comes next.

I had a section at the end of the crisis where they make it to the island – crash into it, just like back in Chapter 1 – and they all run ahead of the Tekeli as it devours the boat and crew. But Cedar, Jack, and Erica wanted to break the prisoners' chains so that they could escape, too. I gave them some rolls to do it before the Tekeli overwhelmed the *Iron Eel*, and they successfully released some people.

But the Tekeli *did* catch up with the NPCs and there was a lot of sanity damage from seeing crew and prisoners savagely torn apart.

Gavril didn't help to free them, but Bryan asked if he could mercy-kill them. Well, dying by a poisoned knife to the neck is better than being ripped apart and chewed up by a shoggoth, so sure. I gave him a skill check and made him sacrifice one dagger per point of success, and Gavril threw away seven knives to give people easier deaths.

So I went ahead and gave the PC group an equal bonus to resist the sanity damage. They no longer had to witness such horrible dismemberment, so they did better against the sanity damage thanks to Gavril. Well done, buddy.

The last part of the race for the temple was fighting through the Dekara. Remember when I said these stock enemies are how the players can measure to see how much more powerful their characters have grown? Well, the PCs did *very* well and kicked a lot of ass. I landed a couple hits against them, but they quickly swept the board clean together, with their teamwork and combos down cold.

The only hiccups were that Cedar's dice hated her for half the fight, and Bryan was determined to use his archery. Gavril wasn't really built for purely ranged combat. He had bonuses for stabbing vital targets and extra damage when he flanked an enemy with an ally. Maybe Bryan was playing it safe by staying back, but cutting half his combat ability meant that he wasn't dishing out top damage and Bryan was frustrated. Nothing I could do about that, but hopefully he'll feel better when he has his big scene with Zoja next.

The Frayed Ends of Sanity

But the player characters still kicked a ton of ass and made it to the temple. This scene was mostly just description, but it's worth noting that as soon as I began describing all the messed-up frescoes and murals, everyone hurried to tell me they kept their eyes on the floor. I silently laughed my ass off as I got to the Cthulhu mosaic on the floor. There was nowhere safe to look.

This final blast to their sanity drove Gavril over the edge for the last time. And he got a critical failure on his sanity defense roll, too, so I decided to give him two derangements for the price of one. Bryan was fine with that – he apparently made a list of his next half dozen derangements just in case.

He selected paranoia because of his experiences in Dunspire, and then pyromania – also because of Dunspire. Fire is now Gavril's answer to anyone who looks at him funny.

Break With Reality

By now, I had Danya speaking entirely Cthyan and Safi was forced to translate for her. Danya was out of her mind, but the group kept following her. They still trusted her!

So I had Danya just ask for the Elder Sign and they put it in her hand, then watched as she walked up to a dark well, talking weird shit about elder gods, and told them "the Elder Sign will draw their attention. If they notice us, they'll destroy all we know."

And then she dropped the Elder Sign into the well. I didn't use the ocean because I wanted a more imminent danger, and it worked perfectly. My players pretty much shit themselves and *no one* saw it coming. Safi did manage to tackle Danya and Kaikoa aced the roll to snatch the Elder Sign.

Sacrifices Must Be Made

It was Zoja who brought poor, screaming Danya back to her senses. Zoja held her axes in front of Danya and told the girl to take them to her mother's fighting school back in Vanhome. Zoja promised that Valtha would teach her.

Holy shit, even after turning on the PCs and almost destroying human civilization on Korvath, they still trusted Danya enough to give her weapons! I *nailed* it!

Cautiously, the characters all let Danya sit up and she took the axes. Zoja asked what she had to do to be the sacrifice. The Tekeli was oozing into the ancient temple after them, so they didn't have a lot of time left.

Danya said the sacrifice only had to be willing. So Zoja took the Elder Sign and told Gavril to make it quick.

I didn't ask Bryan to make a roll to kill Zoja. For one, Zoja wasn't going to fight back. And second, Bryan and Cedar's eyes were both tearing up and I didn't want to risk their big moment with a roll that Bryan might have failed.

So Gavril and Zoja finally finished the battle that began when they first met. Zoja's death lit up the Elder Sign with glowing power. The Tekeli was flooding down into the temple chamber, but then it vanished.

Danya said that using the Sign would not go unnoticed by the elder gods, but... well, someone else will have to deal with that.

An End to Madness

Gavril carried Zoja out of the temple and we had a brief discussion about Antoran burial practices. We agreed that while the ancient Massir and Bhataari may have buried their dead, when everybody lives in mountain cities, there's not enough space to bury people.

Well, maybe except for the occasional ranger murdered for their clothes and hastily buried in the woods.

The Antorans adopted Strazni funeral pyres, so when they got back to The Hunter, Gavril burned Zoja and took both of their payments in salt.

Alak'ai told Gavril that he earned all the salt he could carry and asked where he was going. Gavril answered that he would return to Dunspire to finish burning that place down to the ground. Bryan had visions of Gavril becoming a half-crazed monster hunter, and that sounded like a fitting fate for our assassin.

Safi asked Danya what she would do now. She had Zoja's axes, a promise to keep and a lifelong dream to fulfill. Danya said that she was going to Valtha's fighting school to finish her training.

And then what? With the Tekeli banished, Safi was finally free to return home to Miskaton. But Safi said no, Miskaton wasn't the home she wanted to run back to. Not anymore. She would remain at The Hunter, with Alak and waiting for Danya to come back home to them.

Alak'ai told Kaikoa they had a lot of work to do on the *Iron Eel II*, and then that pretty much wrapped everything up with a neat little bow. Everyone cheered and there were high-fives all around, along with some tears.

It was a good game.

THE END

Tydalus took three times longer to run than I estimated, but we finished the whole thing before Jack had to leave for college and I got to mark another game down in the win column.

In hindsight, I can certainly see a couple of things that I might have changed and improved. The final run-up to the temple went a lot more quickly than I expected, and it would have been a good idea to add a few stages to the sailing and then running crises. Not a whole extra combat or crisis – I was on a timer and didn't want my players to be exhausted for the finale – but some more stages and struggles to evade the encroaching Tekeli would have helped build up the tension.

As a mistake, though, cutting things a little short is better than going too long. Every time that I've had to choose between adding something in to the last session or cutting something out, I always regretted extending the game and been grateful for streamlining.

It's far better to leave your players wanting more, with plenty of energy to pour into their best role-playing during the final scenes of the game, rather than grind through lots of combat and be tired at the climax.

We also got to test out the combo system, and the second draft will need a few changes. For one, most of the abilities that the PCs stacked on enemies with combo didn't end up being useful. The next time that I use the combo rules, rather than adding bleeds and stuns, combo will stack up multiplied damage. The first instance is five extra damage, the second increases that to ten, then twenty, to a max of forty. That's a big dose of damage in our system, so getting a full stack will be really rewarding. But hey, I'm glad we liked combo enough to play with it more.

After Tydalus was all finished, I asked the players for their favorite moments. Every campaign is a learning experience, no matter how many games you've run. I always take note of anything that didn't work – like the sanity restoration I had to adjust in the final chapter – and things that my players liked.

Everyone said that they *loved* lighting Dunspire on fire. But they also liked Ashmont. They got to see two lighthouses, two Antoran towns, and then Dunspire. They were able to compare Kelanua and Antoran life, then see Antoran ways twisted in Dunspire.

Cedar said they got to witness a slice of life on Tydalus and that it was the perfect amount to give her a sense of the entire world. She felt like she had a good understanding of the setting, and in a game that only lasted three months, that's great.

What else did they enjoy? The Tekeli was creepy, which is what I was going for. I borrowed from a mythos that is synonymous with creepy and pulled it off. Cedar also pointed out that ending with a heroic sacrifice coupled with hints that worse things were out there was perfectly genre-appropriate. In cosmic horror, there are always forces beyond human comprehension and every triumph is tainted by the knowledge that humanity is still ultimately doomed.

So I guess I pulled that off, too.

Erica enjoyed getting to try out a polyamorous romance for the first time, and she also liked the priest and his magic in Dunspire. Both she and Cedar said they were surprised by it. They were sunk into the setting enough that they accepted that monsters were out there, but that the unknown belonged down in the sea. Witnessing sorcery in the hands of a human was somehow terrifying.

And Cedar also thanked me for letting her kill Zoja. Not something that a player usually thanks their Storyteller for, but bringing Danya back to herself with their mentor-student and prophetess-follower relationship, and then sacrificing herself so she could go down in history was the perfect closure for Zoja. Especially because Bryan closed the loop on their mysterious first meeting.

I got to give a player the perfect ending for their character, and I loved it, too.

I had a great time running Tydalus. I wish that time had been less of a factor – I probably could have lengthened the campaign without losing any of the story arc and I would have loved to give the player characters more time to interact and develop. But the fact that I ended the game feeling like I wasn't done with Tydalus is a good sign, too. My players and I all want to go back there.

Hopefully, someday we will do just that.

And maybe you will, as well. Whether this campaign is something you're interested in running for your gaming group or not, it was a window into how I create and run my role-playing games. You got a behind-the-scenes look at my world-building, saw my outline at various stages, how crisis scenes and combats can be built. And you watched me make up crises on the spot, deal with unexpected player decisions and course-correct when I made a mistake.

Not every RPG campaign focuses this much on character development and interaction. It's something my gaming group has been doing a long time and has a lot of fun with. There aren't many rules and dice to that part, but hopefully I gave you some idea of how I create those character arcs, form NPC attachments, and set specific moods to evoke reactions from my players. If it's something you do in your games or would like to try out, I hope you have as much fun with it as we did.

Tekeli-li!

For lots more books by Aron Christensen,
visit us at **LLStories.com**

CPSIA information can be obtained
at www.ICGtesting.com
Printed in the USA
BVHW080206180220
572581BV00013B/1913